Hume: A Very Short Introduction

VERY SHORT INTRODUCTIONS are for anyone wanting a stimulating and accessible way into a new subject. They are written by experts, and have been translated into more than 45 different languages.

The series began in 1995, and now covers a wide variety of topics in every discipline. The VSI library currently contains over 650 volumes—a Very Short Introduction to everything from Psychology and Philosophy of Science to American History and Relativity—and continues to grow in every subject area.

Very Short Introductions available now:

Available soon:

For more information visit our website

www.oup.com/vsi/

James A. Harris

HUME

A Very Short Introduction

OXFORD
UNIVERSITY PRESS

OXFORD
UNIVERSITY PRESS

Great Clarendon Street, Oxford, OX2 6DP,
United Kingdom

Oxford University Press is a department of the University of Oxford.
It furthers the University's objective of excellence in research, scholarship,
and education by publishing worldwide. Oxford is a registered trade mark of
Oxford University Press in the UK and in certain other countries

© James A. Harris 2021

The moral rights of the author have been asserted

First edition published in 2021

Impression: 1

Published in the United States of America by Oxford University Press
198 Madison Avenue, New York, NY 10016, United States of America

British Library Cataloguing in Publication Data
Data available

Library of Congress Control Number: 2021936610

ISBN 978-0-19-884978-0

Printed in Great Britain by
Ashford Colour Press Ltd, Gosport, Hampshire

for Florence and Bertie

Contents

Acknowledgements

I am very grateful to friends who took the time to read through the first draft of this book and offer comments and advice that improved it many ways: Donald Ainslie, Michael Gill, Wim Lemmens, Max Skjönsberg, Mark Spencer, and Richard Whatmore. Of course all remaining errors and infelicities are entirely my own responsibility. I benefited also from suggestions made by an anonymous reviewer for Oxford University Press. Jenny Nugee, Luciana O'Flaherty, and the *Very Short Introductions* production team gave me valuable assistance.

I wrote this book at home during the lockdown necessitated by the COVID-19 pandemic in the spring of 2020. That dark and difficult time was made brighter and easier by my family. My wife Jennifer was, as always, supportive and encouraging in every way. Our children Florence and Bertie were extraordinarily cheerful throughout, despite being denied many of the things that they most enjoy in life. Their good humour was an example and an inspiration. Also, I thank Sune, Lotte, David, and Elias Segal for their friendship and hospitality.

List of illustrations

Abbreviations

DNH	*Dialogues concerning Natural Religion* and *The Natural History of Religion*, ed. J. C. A. Gaskin, World's Classics, Oxford University Press, 1993.
E	*Enquiries concerning Human Understanding and the Principles of Morals*. ed. L. A. Selby-Bigge, 3rd edn, revised by P. H. Nidditch, Oxford University Press, 1975.
EMPL	*Essays Moral, Political and Literary*, ed. Eugene F. Miller, revised edition, Liberty Fund, 1987.
HE	*The History of England*, 6 vols, Liberty Fund, 1983.
LDH	*The Letters of David Hume*, ed. J. Y. T. Greig, 2 vols, Oxford University Press, 1932.
T	*A Treatise of Human Nature*, ed. L. A. Selby-Bigge, revised by P. H. Nidditch, Oxford University Press, 1978.

Introduction

In a poll conducted by the BBC in 2005, David Hume was voted the second greatest philosopher of all time. He won more votes than Wittgenstein, Nietzsche, Plato, and Kant, and was beaten only by Karl Marx. Other polls have singled him out as the philosopher of the past with whom present-day philosophers most identify, and as one of the most influential Scots of the past thousand years. This book provides a brief but comprehensive introduction to his thought.

Hume was born in 1711 and died in 1776. He was a contemporary—and friend—of Adam Smith, Jean-Jacques Rousseau, and Benjamin Franklin. He was a central figure in what we now call the European Enlightenment. He was deeply interested in the ancient world, but he also believed that the world he lived in was fundamentally different from ancient Athens and Rome, and he sought to fashion a philosophy that was suitable to modern conditions. This was to be a philosophy that was answerable to the facts of ordinary human experience, that was sceptical of claims made by authority and tradition, that had made its peace with the passions and sentiments. Unusually for his time, Hume believed that it was obvious that the modern world was superior to the ancient, if not always in its art and culture, then certainly in the quality of the lives lived by ordinary human beings. There had, he thought, been undeniable progress in science and government. Thanks largely to the rise of international commerce, people were living freer and happier lives than had ever been possible before. Philosophy, he thought, had a role to play in understanding this process of improvement—and in identifying possible threats to it.

Hume's works are now a staple of university philosophy courses worldwide, and are the subject of a major academic industry. But Hume himself was never a university professor. He was instead what we might now call a public intellectual, and wrote for a wide audience of non-specialists, an audience that included women as well as men. In the 18th century, philosophy was often not so much a distinct subject matter as a particular style of thought, impartial and objective, precise and backed by evidence. It was an age of philosophical religion and philosophical politics, and also of philosophical chemistry and philosophical geology. Hume believed that philosophy defined in this way was vitally important as a means of moderating political, religious, and cultural factionalism. His works taken as a whole can be thought of as a rebuke to the idea that philosophy must be unworldly and disengaged from the concerns of everyday life. They challenge us to think again about what philosophy might have to offer the world outside the walls of the academy.

In 18th-century Britain, those who contributed to intellectual debate tended to be members of the professions. If not university professors, they were church ministers, or lawyers, or physicians. Like another great contemporary, Samuel Johnson, Hume cultivated a wholly new kind of literary identity, that of the independent man of letters, who made his living from his writings alone, and who wrote as his own man, free of obligations either to a patron or to a publisher. Across the Channel, Voltaire had shown what it was possible for a man of letters to achieve, in the way of fame and wealth, given sufficient talent and self-belief. Voltaire also, in an entry to Diderot and d'Alembert's *Encyclopédie*, gave the term 'gens de lettres' a canonical definition. The man of letters was a manifestation of the 'esprit philosophique' of the modern age. He did not aspire towards universal knowledge, yet had the critical and linguistic ability to make any field of study his own. Until recently, the man of learning was kept out of society, secluded in the monastery or university. Now his writings, and his conversation, were a necessary part of social life, and had contributed to the instruction and polish of the nation.

Of all Hume's works, it is his first, *A Treatise of Human Nature*, that has the most secure place on university reading lists today. But the *Treatise* is anomalous in its sheer difficulty, and in the obscurity of its structure and organizing principles. Disappointed by the reception it met with, Hume turned afterwards to the much more popular form of the essay, both as a means of reformatting his theory of human nature, and as the medium for his further explorations of morality and of politics. Following the ancient examples of Plato and Cicero, and the modern examples of Fontenelle and Shaftesbury, he chose the dialogue form for his most profound consideration of the question of what we can know about the first cause of the universe. He also wrote an enormously successful narrative history of England from the Roman invasion to the 'Glorious Revolution' of 1688. All of these texts will be given due attention here.

The reader will find an outline of Hume's career as a man of letters woven into the chapters of this short book. But this is not a biography, and for the full story of Hume's life, it will be necessary to look elsewhere—in the first instance, to Ernest Campbell Mossner's classic *The Life of David Hume*. Our main concern here is with Hume's ideas. We begin with his revolutionary theory of human nature, we move on to his no less strikingly innovative discussions of morality and of politics, and we end with his sceptical and subversive philosophy of religion.

Chapter 1
Human nature

David Hume's first published work, *A Treatise of Human Nature*, originally came in two parts, one on 'the understanding' and the other on 'the passions'. These subjects, Hume told the reader, 'make a compleat chain of reasoning by themselves' (*T* xi). The chain of reasoning concerned a question as old as philosophy itself, the question of the relationship between the rational and the emotional elements of human nature. That relationship had often been depicted in terms of antagonism and combat. Individual happiness and social harmony depended, philosophers had often claimed, on reason winning the battle. In the *Treatise* Hume argued that the whole idea of human nature as site of conflict between reason and passion was a mistake. Properly understood, reason was not a faculty of mind entirely different and distinct in kind from the passions. Reasoning was often, in fact, 'nothing but a species of sensation', a matter merely of 'follow[ing] our taste and sentiment' (*T* 103). But this was nothing to worry about, because, taken as a whole, the passions were able to organize and regulate themselves. It is not impossible that this highly unorthodox conception of the fundamental structure of human nature had its source in Hume's own experience of the implausibility of the traditional account of the reason–passion relationship.

A letter to a physician

Early in September 1729, when he was 18 and still living in the house he had grown up in, Hume suddenly became a mystery to himself. For four years, since he had left college at Edinburgh, he had been engaged in a strenuous and solitary course of study and reflection, with the aim of eventually making his way in the world as a scholar and philosopher. He had worked hard, to the exclusion of almost everything else in life, but he had been happy. Now, though, all his ardour seemed to have deserted him. Suddenly he had no appetite for learning. He felt fine when he put his books to one side, and this made him sure that there was nothing really wrong with him. He was being lazy. He simply needed to work harder. Months passed, and he became aware of physical symptoms indicating that there was more to his condition than mere laziness. He followed the advice of his doctor, took the prescribed medicines, and did more exercise. That helped, he recovered some of his energy, and put on a lot of weight. But in the spring of 1734, four and a half years later, something was still wrong. When he returned to reading and writing, he continued to be dogged by an inability to concentrate. He worried that he would never be able to realize his ambitions. He worried that somehow he had damaged himself with the intensity of his application to his studies. Unable to understand what he was going through, Hume wrote, without revealing his name, to one of the most famous doctors of the day, asking whether his case was a common one, whether he could hope to recover, how long it would take, and how complete a recovery would be (*LDH* i 12–18) (Figure 1).

Hume's endeavours in his teenage years had not been purely speculative. He described to the celebrity physician how he had taken the moral philosophy of ancient Greece and Rome so seriously that he had tried to follow the rigorous mental exercises recommended by writers like Cicero, Seneca, and Plutarch. His

1. From the manuscript of Hume's 1734 letter to an anonymous physician.

goal had been to improve his 'temper' and 'will' as much as his reason and understanding. Young though he was, he had tried to think himself into the frame of mind of the sage who was not bothered by the prospect of death, or poverty, or shame, or pain, or any of the other calamities of life. In retrospect, however, he realized that there had been something not only pointless, but also harmful, in this kind of philosophical regimen. He had not been living an active life, he had been by himself most of the time, and had had, in reality, no reason to fear any of the harms he was steeling himself against. The whole business had been an immense waste of mental energy, and the fact that it had also made him physically ill forced Hume to ask himself if there might not be something fundamentally misconceived in the philosophy according to which he had been trying to live.

The moral philosophy of the ancient world, Hume wrote in his letter, had proceeded on the basis of a set of unexamined assumptions about human nature and about how human beings, possessed of such a nature, ought to go about making themselves happy. Stoic philosophers such as Cicero, Seneca, and Plutarch took it that human beings were most themselves when they were most rational, and that the highest happiness lay in mastering the emotions that got in the way of seeing the world from a properly rational point of view. Hume now found himself doubtful as to whether this really was the truth about how human beings ought to conduct themselves. Life should, of course, be lived in accord with nature. Human nature was the proper point of departure for moral philosophy—and for every other kind of philosophy too. But first it needed to be determined what human nature actually was.

Like many others in Europe at the time, Hume believed that a new era in 'natural philosophy', what we now call natural science, had been announced by Francis Bacon at the beginning of the 17th century. The idea of a fresh start in our knowledge of the natural world had then been made a reality by the work of men such as William Harvey, Robert Boyle, and, especially, Isaac Newton. Through rigorous application of a method grounded in experience and observation, the modern natural philosophers had shown how completely worthless almost all the science of the ancient world was. There had been some 'experimental' work done on human nature already, and in the *Treatise* Hume would acknowledge, in particular, ground-breaking contributions by British philosophers such as John Locke, the third earl of Shaftesbury, Bernard Mandeville, Francis Hutcheson, and Joseph Butler. What he imagined to himself, though, was a comprehensive, systematic analysis of human nature, comparable in its ambition to Newton's great work *The Principles of Natural Philosophy*.

Soon after Hume wrote his letter about his illness and his new intellectual ambition, he left Scotland for the first time. He travelled first to Bristol, where in the employ of a sugar merchant he experimented briefly and apparently unsuccessfully with an active life not devoted to letters and learning. He then crossed the Channel to France. Having spent time in Paris and Rheims, he settled in the small town of La Flèche in Anjou. He seems to have chosen it because it was a cheap place to live, and perhaps because of Scottish connections, rather than because it was where Descartes had gone to college. He would spend three years there working on a theory of human nature that would, so he thought, effect a revolution in philosophy.

Mental anatomy

As Hume understood it, the business of the scientist of human nature was, in the first instance, quite different from that of the moralist who had advice for human beings about how they should live their lives. The moralist could be compared to a painter, whose aim was graceful and engaging depictions of the life of virtue, intended to help people make virtue, not vice, their goal. The kind of work that Hume thought needed to be done, on the other hand, could be compared to that of an anatomist, who began by peeling back the skin and flesh, and whose concern was internal bodily parts that, in themselves, might be hideous to handle and examine. The anatomist's job was not to make the insides of the human body seem beautiful. It was simply to describe the body as it actually was. Similarly, the philosopher of human nature needed to describe what he found in an entirely neutral and objective manner, without making evaluative judgements of any kind. Hume probably took the image of philosophy as anatomy from Mandeville, who in *The Fable of the Bees* had compared 'they that examine into the Nature of Man, abstract from Art and Education' to 'those that study the Anatomy of Dead Carcases'. Mandeville had also claimed that what such mental anatomy showed was that man's 'vilest and most hateful Qualities are the most necessary Accomplishments to fit him for the largest, and according to the World, the happiest and most flourishing Societies'.

It may have been that Hume had developed his early enthusiasm for ancient moral philosophy in the company of Shaftesbury's major work *Characteristicks of Men, Manners, Opinions, Times*. There he would have found an essentially Stoic moral philosophy updated in accord with the literary and aesthetic sensibility of the modern world. Shaftesbury presented the reader with a variety of strategies for self-discovery and for the cultivation of an independence of mind that would provide protection from bodily and worldly evils. The way Hume describes his youthful ambitions to the unnamed doctor makes him sound like one of the many who came under Shaftesbury's influence in the early 18th century. But when he lost his faith in this kind of philosophy, he would have found a kindred spirit in Mandeville, according to whom Shaftesbury was the prime example of a philosopher who thought only of what he wanted himself to be like, and had no awareness at all of his actual nature. 'One of the greatest Reasons why so few People understand themselves,' Mandeville proclaimed, 'is, that most Writers are always teaching Men what they should be, and hardly ever trouble their Heads with telling them what they really are.' Shaftesbury's notions of human nature were a compliment to humankind. What a pity it was that they were not true.

The anatomy of human nature, according to Mandeville, revealed that each human being's mind is, in essence, a 'compound of various Passions', and that these passions control people whether they want them to or not. To look beneath outward appearances is to see that, in their psychology as in their physiology, human beings are not very different from the rest of the animal kingdom. The fact that human beings, unlike animals, live in large political and commercial societies can be explained without recourse to the supposition of any uniquely human capacities. Hume, too, believed that an 'anatomical' approach to human nature revealed fundamental similarities between human beings and animals. The major defect of the systems of the mind developed by philosophers was, he thought, that they tended to suppose that the concerns and aptitudes of philosophers provide insight into human nature as such. To focus on the similarities between human minds and animal minds was a salutary corrective to the distortions that such a supposition introduced into the science of human nature.

Another key influence on Hume's study of human nature was Locke's *Essay concerning Human Understanding*. Like Locke, Hume imagined that in the beginning, at the time of our birth, the mind is a blank sheet, completely empty of ideas, waiting to be filled by the results of sensory contact with the outside world. Of course, there are basic principles of mental functioning which inform how the mind operates on the inputs from the senses. But all of our notions and beliefs, and all but the most elementary of our desires, are the product of experience. To make sense of ourselves, then, it was necessary to try to reconstruct how mental life as we know it might have developed by way of the accumulation of, and interaction between, an almost infinite number of individual perceptions and sensations. It was pointless, however, to involve actual physiology in the attempt to discover order in the apparent chaos of the inner life. To do that was inevitably to get caught up in fraught debates about the relation between mind and body which had dogged the philosophy of the 17th century, and which Locke's purely experience-based method enabled his followers to put to one side. Locke had transformed the study of the mind and its powers by sticking resolutely to that method, particularly insofar as he had identified the limits of what the understanding enables us to understand. Hume began his anatomy of human nature with further examination of the understanding, and with the apparent discovery that it is even less reliable than Locke had imagined.

The understanding

One of the earliest of Hume's surviving letters tells us that at the same time that he was planning a new, anatomical, science of human nature, he was reading the French sceptic Pierre Bayle (*LDH* i 12). In a devastating critique of the moral casuistry of mainstream French Catholic culture, Bayle had revived styles of argument characteristic of ancient Pyrrhonism, a school of extreme scepticism intent on showing that no proposition can be proved any more likely to be true than its negation. His goal had been to undermine the whole idea of a rational Christianity such as could be taught in schools and seminaries, and to show that the foundation of true religion had to be a faith given directly to human beings by God himself. Confidence in reason, in other words, was completely unjustified. Such confidence was likely to lead to error, and sin. Hume did not share Bayle's religious objectives, but he was deeply impressed by the French philosopher's assault on the pretensions of philosophy. During his time in La Flèche, he would have had access to the library of the college there, and could have read widely and deeply in its collection of both ancient and modern sceptical texts. Pyrrhonist themes are woven into many of Hume's writings, nowhere more strikingly than in the theory of the human understanding laid out in Book One of *A Treatise of Human Nature*, the dramatic culmination of which is a cry of despair in the face of what looked like a choice 'betwixt a false reason and none at all' (*T* 268).

The first step towards this apocalyptic conclusion was an investigation into the workings of the understanding in its everyday guise, as the means by which human beings make judgements about the world that lies beyond the bounds of their immediate experience. Philosophers—with the notable exception of Locke—had traditionally restricted their attention to how it is that we are able to achieve absolute certainty, in mathematics and other kinds of pure enquiry where it is possible to demonstrate that such-and-such *must* be true. Hume was more interested in probabilistic judgements about matters of contingent fact: that is, in the judgements that we make, using our experience, about how the future will be, how things might have been in the past, and what might explain what is happening in the world now. This was the ordinary business of ordinary people reflecting on matters of ordinary concern. But it was also, albeit in a much more carefully regimented manner, the business of natural scientists trying to make better sense of the world around us, and the business too of anatomists of human nature trying to make sense of the world within us. What Hume wanted to know was *how* the understanding enables us to form beliefs about what the weather will be like tomorrow, about why our army lost the battle, and about how rainbows appear in the sky.

Such beliefs, Hume decided, are all beliefs about causes and effects. We are able to analyse our experiences in a variety of ways, in terms for example of what resembles or is identical with what, in terms of how things are related in time and space, and in terms of proportion and degree and contrariety. But it is the causal relation 'that can be trac'd beyond our senses, and informs us of existences and objects, which we do not see or feel' (*T* 74). And what Hume discovered as he examined how it is that we form beliefs about causes and effects was that reason, in one important sense of the word, is not involved. When we form a belief about tomorrow on the basis of what has regularly happened in the past, we do not make use of any general principle that would entitle us to say that we are using the past to *prove* that tomorrow this is more likely to take place than that. To be entitled to say such a thing, we would have to combine a description of how things have been in the past with confidence that the laws of nature never change. Then, and only then, would we be entitled to use past experience to make a rational inference about the future.

The problem is that there is no way of proving that the laws of nature never change. Our only basis for what we believe about the laws of nature is, after all, our past experience. And we cannot use that to prove that our past experience is a reliable guide to how things will be in the future. Nor is there any way of abstracting from experience to prove that it just must be the case, as a matter of metaphysical or logical necessity, that the laws of nature never change. For we can imagine that the laws of nature might have been different from what we have experienced them to be.

There is then no possible source for a general principle concerning the immutability of the laws of nature. That means that our causal beliefs have to be explained without recourse to such a principle. And *that* means, Hume concluded, that when we form beliefs about the future on the basis of the past, we are not making inferences and drawing conclusions. Rather, the mental processes involved are mere habits of association, whereby some regularly experienced conjunction of events prompts us to believe that, for example, a cloudy sky will soon be followed by rain. When we open the curtains and see a grey sky outside, the idea that it will rain before long just feels more compelling—as Hume puts it, it has more 'vivacity'—than the idea that we are in for a long hot day of sunshine. It was not reason but rather custom that was, Hume claimed, 'the guide of life' (*T* 652).

This discovery of the centrality to our cognitive lives of automatic associations of ideas was what Hume himself took to be his primary contribution to the science of human nature. It did not mean that we form our beliefs about the world in a blind and random manner. On the contrary, it was plain that there are principles or rules by means of which the formation of causal beliefs is generally and naturally regulated. For instance, we tend to assume that, as Hume put it, '[t]he same cause always produces the same effect, and the same effect never arises but from the same cause' (*T* 173). But the ubiquity of patterns of association in

13

our thought about the future and past did mean that we have no obvious reason to pride ourselves on possessing a special faculty of reason that distinguishes us from and elevates us above the rest of the animal kingdom. Just like the other animals, we rely on custom and habit, not rational insight into the unchangeability of nature, in our decisions about how to respond to the world around us.

That was an unnerving conclusion to reach, but, in itself, it did not mean that our natural belief-forming processes were untrustworthy. Worries about the reliability of the understanding arose only when Hume realized that, properly speaking, we have no idea at all what we are talking about when we call one thing the cause of another. We come to believe that one thing is the cause of another when the two things in question have presented themselves in our experience in a particular way. They have regularly come into contact with each other, one thing comes before the other in order of time, and they have been constantly conjoined with each other such that one thing never appears without being followed by the other. But to say that the first thing is the *cause* of the second is to say more than this. It is to say that there is some means by which the first thing *makes* the second thing happen. It is to say that there is some kind of necessary connection between the two things, such that given the first thing, the second *must* happen. And, Hume argued, we have no insight into whatever it might be that necessarily connects a cause with its effect. All we have experience of is the constant conjunction. When we talk of the power that a cause has to *make* the effect take place, we are merely projecting onto the world the sense we have that the effect definitely will follow the cause.

The very idea of one thing being the cause of another appeared, therefore, to be the product of an illusion of the imagination. And Hume could not help worrying about whether we should allow ourselves to be guided by such illusions. 'Nothing', he reminded himself, 'is more dangerous to reason than flights of the imagination, and nothing has been the occasion of more mistakes among philosophers' (*T* 267). So perhaps the philosopher should reject the promptings of the imagination, and believe only what he could be absolutely certain about. The problem was that it was fairly easy to show that, when subjected to critical reflection, all certainty degenerates into mere probability, and that probability diminishes to the point where there could be no confidence at all in the matter under consideration. It was a matter of ordinary experience that no one is so confident of his powers of reasoning that he does not accept that sometimes he makes mistakes. But any judgement about the chance of an error in a particular case had to go along with an acceptance that that judgement itself could be erroneous. And a judgement of the likelihood of error about that could, in turn, be mistaken. And so on.

It was at this point that Hume found himself apparently faced with a choice between, on the one hand, a 'false', or deceptive, reason, in the form of a reason that was merely a disposition of the associative imagination, and, on the other hand, a reason that was 'no reason at all' because it destroyed confidence in every single one of his judgements and beliefs. It looked as if Bayle and the Pyrrhonists were right, and that the rational thing to do was to accept the sceptical conclusion and suspend judgement altogether. Yet this, Hume quickly discovered, was impossible. In reality he had no choice but, at some point, to look up from his desk, leave his study, re-engage with the world, and carry on forming beliefs, and acting on them, like everyone else. And as soon as he did so, the philosophical arguments that had made him lose confidence in his everyday habits of mind looked absurd. 'I dine, I play a game of back-gammon, I converse, and am merry with my friends', Hume reflected; 'and when after three or four hours' amusement, I wou'd return to these speculations, they appear so cold, and strain'd, and ridiculous, that I cannot find in my heart to enter into them any farther' (*T* 269).

The whole project of an accurate and anatomical examination of human nature—in fact, of anything at all—looked as though it had run into the sand. But Hume found that there was a part of him that wanted to carry on regardless. And this undimmed curiosity was sufficient to make him sceptical about the scepticism he had reasoned himself into. In other words, it made him sceptical about the philosophical reasoning that had, for a moment, robbed him of his confidence in the power of understanding that he would have to rely on in his further investigations into human nature. Perhaps it did not matter that it was not possible to *prove* that his understanding was reliable in the judgements it made and the beliefs it formed. Perhaps the philosopher should simply accept his essentially animal nature, and submit to the involuntary cognitive processes that he shared with every other human being. He had no insight into the real nature of causal powers, nor into whatever it was that was responsible for the laws of nature being what they were. But this did not stop him forming beliefs about causal connections in nature; nor did it seem to be a reason not to indulge his desire to know more about the things that interested him most: 'the principles of moral good and evil, the nature and foundation of government, and the cause of those several passions and inclinations, which actuate and govern me' (*T* 271).

The passions

Hume had discovered that the understanding, the special activity which philosophers had fixed upon to define human beings and to distinguish them from the other animals, was, in reality, the work of habitual and automatic associations of ideas. The associative imagination took the felt vivacity of the perceptions of the senses, and transferred it to ideas of the causes and effects of those perceptions, thereby giving those ideas a felt firmness or strength that distinguished them from mere conceptions and fancies. Thus the various different kinds of mental activity—perceiving, conjecturing, remembering, judging, believing—were distinguished simply by how they felt, rather than by being based in autonomous faculties of the mind. The cognitive dimension of human nature was constructed and animated by the ebb and flow of these feelings. This meant that it no longer looked plausible to suppose that the human mind was structured by a categorical division between reason on the one hand and emotion on the other. The traditional distinction between reason and feeling had collapsed, to the extent that reasoning was in itself, as Hume put it, 'nothing but a wonderful and unintelligible instinct in our souls' (*T* 179).

It followed that the dynamics of the practical life had to be reconceived along the same lines. 'Nothing is more usual in philosophy, and even in common life', Hume noted, 'than to talk of the combat of passion and reason' (*T* 413). Most moral philosophy, both ancient and modern, had been founded on a way of thinking according to which we are obliged to regulate our actions by reason and to oppose and subdue any passions which pose a challenge to reason's authority. This was the way of thinking that Hume, in his letter to the physician, described himself as having subscribed to in his youth. It was, Hume now saw, a way of thinking that was fundamentally mistaken. The combat between practical reason and passion is in fact a combat between different kinds of passions, between passions that feel so 'calm' that we mistake them for acts of reason, and 'violent' passions that are as uncomfortable and disruptive as all passions are usually supposed to be. It is not a combat that the violent passions are bound to win, because violence is not the same thing as strength. It is perfectly possible for a calm passion to be so deeply embedded in a person's nature that it is able to resist the pushes and pulls of the violent passions. This, and not success in the techniques of self-mastery, was what philosophers were talking about when they talked about the government of the passions by reason.

Questions immediately arose however. Without a faculty of reason empowered to discipline and control the passions, how exactly was their violence to be overcome? How was strength of mind, the prevalence of the calm passions over the violent, to be achieved? What, if anything, made it possible to establish order, in human nature, and in society at large?

These were especially pressing questions for Hume because the passions that are most salient in his anatomy of human nature are intrinsically violent passions like pride, shame (Hume's word is 'humility'), love, and hatred. These are the passions that had been of most interest to Mandeville too, but Hume would have also found them thoroughly explored in 17th-century French moralists such as Blaise Pascal, the duc de la Rochefoucauld, and Jean de la Bruyère. They are passions that were supposed by these writers to set human beings at odds both with themselves and with other people. In England Thomas Hobbes had described pride, or 'glory', as one of the 'principall causes of quarrell' which turns man's natural condition into a state of war of every man against every man. Hume believed that animals as well as human beings feel pride, shame, love, and hatred. But animals do not live in intensely competitive commercial societies in which the struggle for status and recognition is as intense as the struggle for survival. It mattered then, that, having removed a controlling faculty of reason from human nature, Hume had an account to give of how the violent passions are tamed and suppressed.

Pride, shame, love, and hatred are classified by Hume as 'indirect' passions. They are different in kind from simple and immediate responses to present or future good and evil, like joy and sorrow, or hope and fear. Their indirectness lies in the fact that they are complex mental phenomena which arise from ideas of ourselves in our relations with a wide variety of causes of pleasure and pain. I feel pride, for example, when a cause of pleasure is related in some more or less intimate way to me. I feel love for you—the kind of love that might also be called 'esteem'—when a cause of pleasure is related in the same kind of way to you. The object, or focus, of pride is, Hume claimed, always myself, just as the object or focus of love was always another person. That is just a basic feature of how the mind works. But the fact that so many different things can be causes of pride and esteem—our possessions as well as all kinds of personal merit and accomplishment—implied that the causation of the indirect passions is not in each case the work of an innate and specific principle of mind, but is rather to be understood in terms of the particular instantiation of quite general laws of mental functioning. Hume was especially interested in how the relation of ownership, or property, insinuates itself into our emotional lives to the point where it is the principal cause of these 'indirect' passions. He was, after all, living in a world in which 'houses, equipage, furniture, cloaths, horses, [and] hounds' (*T* 310) appeared to matter as much, if not more, than anything else in life.

The hold of the indirect passions upon us is strengthened by the fact that they are intensely *social*. My pride in my fine house, for example, is immeasurably heightened by my awareness of the esteem that you and everyone else feels for me as its owner. Hume explained our responsiveness to the feelings and opinions of others in terms of 'that propensity we have to sympathise with others, and to receive by communication their inclinations and sentiments, however different from, or even contrary to our own' (*T* 316). Sympathy—not here a form of compassion, but rather a kind of attunement to the states of mind of other people—is absolutely central to the world of the passions as Hume describes it. It gives us the vivid, sometimes pleasurable, sometimes painful, sense we always have of ourselves as standing in relation with other people. It makes the human condition a condition of unavoidable sociability. It explains why man is 'the creature of the universe, who has the most ardent desire of society, and is fitted for it by the most advantages'. After all, '[w]e can form no wish, which has not a reference to society. A perfect solitude is, perhaps, the greatest punishment we can suffer' (*T* 363).

Sympathy combines with our interest in property to generate a form of love or esteem which Hume took to be particularly prevalent in human nature. This is the admiration we feel for the rich and powerful. Such admiration, he observed, is usually unconnected to an expectation that we might personally benefit from the wealth and influence of those we look up to. Our esteem for riches is generally disinterested, just like our contempt for indigence and poverty. Sympathy explains this otherwise mysterious phenomenon. It makes sense of why we take vicarious pleasure in the pleasure taken by the rich and powerful in their riches and power. And in the process it goes some way towards explaining why highly stratified societies are not pulled apart by tensions arising from inequalities of wealth and social standing. Of course there is bound to be resentment and envy on the part of the poor and powerless when they compare their lives with the lives of their superiors. But, Hume suggested, this resentment usually produces not a desire to overturn the social order, but, instead, a desire on the part of the lower orders to improve their situation relative to those around them. For we care much more about how we stand in our relations with our peers than about the distance between us and the rich and famous.

In his analysis of the passions Hume's attitude was self-consciously that of the cool and objective anatomist. He made no value judgements about the way in which human beings show themselves to be just as concerned about their property as about their virtue. The prominence of pride in human life, fixed upon as a sign of corruption and sinfulness by the French moralists of the 17th century, and by Scottish Calvinists too, was merely described, and not judged. The same goes for our obsession with the lives and possessions of the rich and powerful, and for the distaste we feel at the sight of poverty and degradation. Instead, Hume went to great lengths to show how the associative model of the mind that he had sketched in his account of the understanding could be developed so as to apply also to the myriad complexities of the emotional life. It is here that his ambition to put the science of the mind on a rigorously experimental footing, so that it might be comparable in explanatory sophistication to the science of nature, is most obvious. Hume seized on 'experiments to confirm this system' and displayed them in the minutest detail. He was especially proud of having identified a 'double relation of ideas and impressions' that explained every operation of every indirect passion, no matter what the cause of the passion was taken to be: in every case, '[t]hat cause, which excites the passion, is related to the object, which nature has attributed to the passion; the sensation, which the cause separately produces, is related to the sensation of the passion' (*T* 286).

Working in this spirit, Hume did not make it his business to give advice about how the passions should be regulated, so that the violent passions were contained and controlled. This was theoretical, not practical, philosophy. As such, it was a philosophy wholly different in kind to that which Hume had experimented with in his teenage years. But it was, at the same time, a philosophy which addressed the problem that practical moralists had always concerned themselves with, the problem of the government of the passions. The startling message of Hume's theory of the passions was that the passions could be left to govern themselves. This was what the centrality of sympathy to the emotional life made it possible to conceive. For sympathy ensures that my pride, esteem, and so forth are attuned to yours, so that a process of accommodation and moderation goes on all the time, as each one of us seeks the social satisfactions they crave. Human nature, on this picture, is to a significant extent defined by the social contexts in which human beings always live. '[T]he minds of men are mirrors to one another' (*T* 365), Hume remarked, and just as mirrors are not in control of the reflections they give, so also our feelings, and beliefs, cannot help but be impinged upon by the feelings and beliefs of those around us. This was why Hobbes had been wrong in his claim that the natural state of human beings is a state of permanent antagonism and conflict.

That said, there were even so obvious limits to our sympathetic sociability—limits that, at last, brought into view a fundamental difference between human beings and the other animals. The societies that human beings live in are so large and complex that peace and order require the invention of moral codes, and of government and political power too.

Second thoughts?

Hume left La Flèche in the summer of 1737. He travelled to London, in order to find a publisher for his new system of the understanding and the passions. *A Treatise of Human Nature* appeared in the book shops in January 1739, with a subtitle describing it as 'An Attempt to Introduce the Experimental Method of Reasoning into Moral Subjects'. (By 'moral subjects' Hume meant matters that were, as Samuel Johnson put it in his *Dictionary*, 'such as [are] known or admitted in the general business of life', as distinct from the more exact and rarefied concerns of *natural* philosophy.) On the title-page (Figure 2) Hume put an ambiguous motto from Tacitus: '*Rara temporum felicitas, ubi sentire quæ velis; & quæ sentias, dicere licet*' ['Rare happiness of the times, when you may think as you will, and speak as you think']. Was Hume saying that he was glad to have been able to follow his anatomical argument where it led him, and not to have had to pretend to share the didactic concerns of the moralizing 'painter'? Or was he hinting that there was more he wanted to say, but felt unable to put into print? Were there, for example, religious implications to his theory of human nature that he was unwilling, for the moment at least, to spell out? To many of his readers, Hume's silence about, for example, the role of God's grace in the regulation of the passions would have been deafening.

The *Treatise* contains much more than it has been possible to describe here. One of the four 'parts' of Book One on the understanding concerns our ideas of space and time, and whether time and space can be divided into ultimately indivisible parts. Hume's treatment of probabilistic reasoning by itself stretches over almost 200 pages. It is followed by a comprehensive

A
TREATISE
OF
Human Nature :

BEING

An ATTEMPT to introduce the experimental Method of Reasoning

INTO

MORAL SUBJECTS.

*Rara temporum felicitas, ubi sentire, quæ velis ; & quæ
sentias, dicere licet.* TACIT.

VOL. I.

OF THE
UNDERSTANDING.

LONDON:
Printed for JOHN NOON, at the *White-Hart*, near
Mercer's-Chapel, in *Cheapside.*

MDCCXXXIX,

2. The title-page of *A Treatise of Human Nature.*

treatment of 'the sceptical and other systems of philosophy' that takes in, among other things, the origins of the belief in an external world, the metaphysics of material nature, and the basis of the idea of a single self that stays the same through time. Book Two's application to the passions of the experimental method of reasoning is exhaustive and sometimes exhausting in its attention to the minutiae of the economy of the emotions. It enumerates the wide range of different causes of pride and shame and of love and hatred. It analyses in detail how a variety of factors increases and decreases the violence of passions. Along the way, Hume examines the age-old question of whether freedom of action is compatible with the necessitation of choice by motives. He argues that it is. The contrary view—what philosophers today call 'incompatibilism'—is motivated by a misunderstanding of causal necessity. Once necessity is redefined along the lines argued for in Book One of the *Treatise*, the problem, so we are told, simply disappears.

It is not at all clear how, or whether, everything in the *Treatise* fits together into a single coherent line of argument. Soon after it was published, Hume brought out a brief 'abstract', or summary, intended to draw attention to his principal discoveries. These, he believed, were the treatment of probable reasoning, and the role he ascribed to the associative imagination. In 1748 he published a completely rewritten version of Book One, entitled *Philosophical Essays concerning Human Understanding*. Later he changed the title to *An Enquiry concerning Human Understanding*. As in the abstract of the *Treatise*, the focus in the *Enquiry* was exclusively upon Hume's new account of reasoning about matters of empirical fact, along with its sceptical implications for insight into the relation between causes and effects. 'By shortening & simplifying the Questions', he told a friend, 'I really render them much more complete. *Addo dum minuo* [I add by taking away]' (*LDH* i 158). Then in 1757 he published a greatly stripped down 'Dissertation on the Passions'. It further emphasized Hume's view that the passions are 'susceptible of as accurate a disquisition, as the laws of motion, optics, hydrostatics, or any part of natural philosophy'.

The question raised by the way Hume repackaged the arguments of the *Treatise* in later works is whether it implies that he had lost confidence in the parts of his first book that disappeared from view as a result. No second edition of the *Treatise* ever appeared, and late in life Hume wrote an 'Advertisement' for his collected philosophical works which disowned it as a 'juvenile work, which the Author never acknowledged' (*E* 2). 'I was carried away by the Heat of Youth & Invention to publish too precipitately,' he explained in the letter quoted from above. 'So vast an Undertaking, plan'd before I was one and twenty, & compos'd before twenty five, must necessarily be very defective. I have repented my Haste a hundred & a hundred times.' But what, exactly, was it that he came to repent? The streamlining of argument in the *Enquiry concerning Human Understanding* suggests that, at the very least, he regretted having tried to do too many things at once. The *Treatise* does not give the impression that its author was in complete control of his text. Sometimes one has the sense that Hume wanted above all to collect together every good idea and argument he had ever thought of, without concern for principles of narrative order and logical architecture.

It is possible that Hume also came to worry that the scepticism on display in Book One of the *Treatise* lent itself to misinterpretation, as if he were actually endorsing the extreme doubt that he so dramatically articulates at the conclusion of his examination of the understanding. Take, for instance, his treatment of belief in an external world in the section 'Of scepticism with regard to the senses'. Hume begins by asserting that it is pointless to ask whether or not things really exist outside the mind. 'That is a point', he insists, 'which we must take for granted in all our reasonings' (*T* 187). Yet when he has completed his long investigation into the causes which prompt us to believe in the continuing and independent existence of material objects, he finds himself no longer so sure. For the perceptions on the basis of which we construct the world of experience have none of the coherence and constancy that we attribute to their supposedly objective and enduring causes. Neither sense perception itself nor reason is able to explain belief in an external world. Only the imagination can explain it, and, as in the case of causal reasoning, the means by which the imagination does its work here are not such as to inspire confidence in the result. At the end of the section Hume admits that he 'cannot conceive how such trivial qualities of the fancy, conducted by such false suppositions, can ever lead to any solid or rational system' (*T* 217). Taking everything into account, he now feels more inclined to place no confidence at all in his senses than to maintain the implicit trust that he started out with.

Was Hume saying, then, that the rational thing to do was not to believe in an external world? Was he setting philosophy against common sense and ordinary belief, and forcing the reader to choose between them? Was this the real message of Book One of the *Treatise*? Was the talk in the final section of the curative properties of backgammon and dining with friends no more than an attempt to disguise where the argument really led? In the *Enquiry* Hume appears keen to make it clear that this is *not* how he should be read. A very brief summary of 'Of scepticism with regard to the senses' is introduced at the end of the book as an instance of 'excessive scepticism', the kind of argumentation that might appear plausible in the classroom or study, but that is immediately subverted by 'action, and employment, and the occupations of common life' (*E* 159). Pyrrhonism is, by definition, useless. It cannot be put into practice, for it undermines the very basis of action as such. Hume does not say here that there is anything wrong, logically speaking, with extreme scepticism. But he does do his best to put distance between it and *moderate* scepticism. Moderate scepticism is 'durable and useful' (*E* 161). It reminds us of the limited nature of our intellectual faculties, and enjoins us to restrict our enquiries to subject matters which those faculties are suited to. This, Hume wanted the reader to believe, is the kind of scepticism that issues from his account of the understanding.

Uniformity and difference

As he changed his mind about how his theory of human nature should be presented to the reader, Hume did not give up on the idea that there really is such a thing as a single human nature, shared by all human beings in all times and all places. All human beings, he was sure, reason in the same way about their lives and the world around them. All human beings are subject to the passions of pride, shame (or 'humility'), love, and hatred. 'It is universally acknowledged', Hume claimed in the *Enquiry concerning Human Understanding*, 'that there is a great uniformity among the actions of men, in all nations and ages, and that human nature remains still the same, in its principles and operations' (*E* 83). Yet this was compatible, Hume wanted to insist, with the fact that human life is different in different times and places. It was still possible to talk, as people in the 18th century liked to do, of countries as having distinctive 'national characters', such that particular sets of habits, manners, and morals are more frequently met with in one people than among their neighbours. In his essay 'Of National Characters' Hume argued that his theory of sympathy provided an explanation of national particularity, and that therefore it was not necessary to appeal, as many (including Montesquieu) did, to 'physical causes' such as climate, soil, and landscape.

National character could change through time. Hume's *History of England* was, in part, a study of how English—and indeed European—manners had changed with the decline of feudalism and the rise of manufacturing and commerce. However, when Hume looked beyond Europe, his historical imagination failed him. What he saw as a lack of achievement in manufacturing, arts, and sciences elsewhere in the world suggested to him that there are different 'kinds' or 'species' of men, and that non-Europeans are 'naturally inferior to the whites'. As purported evidence for this repellent proposition, Hume observes that 'there are Negroe [*sic*] slaves dispersed all over Europe, of whom none ever discovered any symptoms of ingenuity; though low people, without education, will start up amongst us, and distinguish themselves in every profession' (*EMPL* 208 fn.). Somehow it did not occur to Hume that there might be non-biological causes, in the form of grotesquely inhumane treatment, that might explain what slaves of African origin were and were not able to achieve when they found themselves among Europeans. His endorsement of innate racial difference was picked up and used by such defenders of slavery as the plantation owner Edward Long in his 1774 *History of Jamaica*.

It is hard not to feel that, despite its pretensions to universalism, Hume's interest in 'human nature' was really an interest in human beings as they conducted themselves in the particular kind of society, modern commercial society, in which he happened to live. The slave trade, of course, did much to make that kind of society possible. As in England and France, merchants and investors in Scotland became vastly wealthy through profits made in the Caribbean plantations to which hundreds of thousands of African slaves were transported. But Hume found almost nothing to say about modern slavery. It is mentioned in his works only once, in the context of a discussion of whether or not the modern world was more populous than the ancient (see *EMPL* 429). Hume, like almost all of his contemporaries, averted his eyes from this part of the substructure of commercial society, and concentrated his attention on, as he put it himself, 'men's behaviour in company, in affairs, and in their pleasures' (*T* xxiii).

Chapter 2
Morality

Hume's theory of human nature was initially intended to be the foundation for 'a system of the sciences'. The system would comprise analyses of morals, 'criticism' (what we now call aesthetics), and politics. When complete, it would amount to a full examination of 'almost every thing, which it can in any way import us to be acquainted with, or which can tend either to the improvement or ornament of the human mind' (*T* xx). But after he had finished his account of morality, in Book Three of the *Treatise*, Hume gave up on the whole project, and renounced aspirations to systematicity. He turned instead to writing brief and elegant essays on miscellaneous moral and political topics. He also changed his literary persona. No longer merely an 'anatomist' of human affairs, he now allowed himself to be read as seeking to have a positive, improving influence on manners and morals. The culmination of Hume's experiment with the combination of anatomy and 'painting' was *An Enquiry concerning the Principles of Morals*, the book which he would judge to the best of all of his writings.

Fragments of a system of the sciences

While he waited to see what the literary world would make of the first instalment of *A Treatise of Human Nature*, Hume finished Book Three, 'Of Morals'. The principal question to be addressed in his treatment of morality had been introduced already, in Book Two, when he mentioned 'the controversy, which of late years has so much excited the curiosity of the publick, *whether ... moral distinctions be founded on natural and original principles, or arise from interest and education*' (*T* 295). This was a question which Mandeville's writings, in particular, had made pressing. In his major work, *The Fable of the Bees*, Mandeville had argued that no moral distinctions are founded on natural principles, and that all arise from interest and education. Human beings, according to Mandeville, are not naturally sociable creatures. They have to be manipulated and coerced into cooperating with each other and respecting authority, and the invention of moral rules and institutions is an essential part of this process of socialization. In his discussion in Book Two of virtue and vice as the causes of pride and 'humility', Hume had put the question of the naturalness of morality to one side. Now, though, equipped as he was with a worked-out theory of human nature, he was in a position to address it head on.

His answer was that, while some of morality has a basis in natural principles, important parts of it do not. A large part of Book Three of the *Treatise* is given over to arguments intended to prove that the virtue of justice, in particular, is artificial. By 'justice' Hume meant respect for rights of property, and for the rules which determine how property is transferred from one person to another, as well as for the contracts which make it possible for transfers of property in the future to be guaranteed by actions taken by one party in the present. Rules fixing the distinction between possession and property, and the conveyance of property between individuals, are essential to the peaceful social life of human beings. But, Hume argued, they are not rules that human beings are naturally disposed to follow or to regard as morally obligatory. A reliable respect for them depends in the first instance upon a disciplined regulation of self-interest such as can only be inculcated through upbringing, education, and societal pressure. As obedience to the rules becomes a matter of second nature, so the sense arises in each individual that there is a distinctively moral value to such obedience. Sympathy attunes them to the benefits of the rules to society at large. In this way the limits of natural sympathetic sociability are extended, and human beings learn to accommodate themselves to the needs and expectations of all members of society.

Similarly artificial, Hume argued, is the sense of an obligation to obey the state simply because it is the state, regardless of one's views about the characters and aims of those who happen to possess political power. In the wake of the social contract theories of Hobbes and Locke, that was not a very controversial claim to make—though, as we will see in Chapter 3, Hume was highly critical of how the contractarians themselves explained the basis of political obligation. Much more unpalatable to his contemporaries was Hume's further claim that, similarly, there is nothing natural in a woman's obligation to chastity. But Mandeville was mistaken to go so far as to claim that *all* of morality is artificial. There are virtues that have no dependence on artifice and contrivance. There are character traits that naturally elicit esteem, or contempt, without having to be seen in the context of systems of conventions that make extensive human society possible. The benefits are obvious of such virtues as '[m]eekness, beneficence, charity, generosity, clemency, moderation, [and] equity' (*T* 578). The 'natural humanity' that prompts us to act in these ways is plainly something to be admired and cherished, in each and every case of its exercise.

In his inaugural lecture as professor of moral philosophy at the University of Glasgow, Francis Hutcheson had countered Mandeville by insisting that 'the best of the ancient writers' were right in their view that virtue is 'the best and most perfect life according to nature'. Hume sought to find a way between Mandeville on the one hand and Hutcheson on the other. Hutcheson was well known for having claimed, in answer to Mandeville, that human beings possess a special 'moral sense', by means of which they distinguish between virtue and vice without any consideration of self-interest. By the same token, Hutcheson had argued in earlier writings, it was obvious that it is wrong to claim, as some philosophers had, that moral judgements are the work of a faculty of pure reason, comparable in their certainty to proofs in mathematics and logic. Hume agreed with Hutcheson that morals are not matters of pure reason. This was obvious from the fact that moral judgements 'excite passions, and produce or prevent actions' (*T* 457). Even so, Hume was not prepared to accept the existence of a special 'moral sense' comparable to the senses of sight, hearing, and smell. (The fact that he gave a section of Book Three the title 'Moral distinctions deriv'd from a moral sense' is therefore misleading.) Hutcheson was right to have objected to Mandeville that distinctively moral ideas of approval and disapproval cannot be reduced to judgements of self-interest. But those ideas could be explained in other terms. The capacity for sympathy that Hume appealed to in his analysis of the passions provided a means of understanding them as pleasurable and painful responses to the pleasures and pains of other people. Morality could be explicated in terms of utility, supplemented, Hume argued, by ideas of what was 'agreeable'.

To reject the idea that the making of moral distinctions is the work of reason was not to embrace an extreme subjectivism. Neither Hutcheson nor Hume was saying that there is no possibility of error in moral judgement. It is true that, as Hume put it, 'when you pronounce any action or character to be vicious, you mean nothing, but that from the constitution of your nature you have a feeling or sentiment of blame from the contemplation of it' (*T* 469). In other words, you mean that you have a feeling or sentiment of displeasure and uneasiness. But this does not detract from the reality of vice, or of virtue. Moral judgements can be compared to judgements about sounds, colours, smells, and heat and cold. Modern philosophers like Locke had established that such 'secondary qualities' were, in Hume's words, 'not qualities in objects, but perceptions in the mind' (*T* 469). But, of course, it remained the case that I could be wrong when I judged that something was blue not red, or sweet not sour. Almost all people, given the right conditions, agree when it comes to colour, or flavour. Disagreement can usually be explained by poor light or distance, or temporary or permanent damage to the sense of taste. In morals, too, a standard of correctness is provided by the normal functioning of the faculty of sympathy, which is to say, by general agreement as to what is praiseworthy and blameworthy.

Hume's plan had been to move on from morality to further books of the *Treatise* on 'criticism' and on politics. As it turned out, though, Book Three marked the end of Hume's projected 'system of the sciences'. He went on to write a great deal about politics, in essays and in *The History of England*. But about criticism, and the principles of artistic taste, he wrote comparatively little. It is not clear why. Hume's letters, as well as a profusion of references in his published works, tell us that he was deeply interested in the arts, especially in literature and history, ancient and modern. The earliest of his surviving letters describes him reading Milton and Virgil. On his deathbed he read the Greek satirist Lucian and the recently published first volume of Gibbon's *Decline and Fall of the Roman Empire*. Yet Hume did not attempt anything on the scale of, for example, his friend Lord Kames's two-volume *Elements of Criticism*, or the Aberdeen professor George Campbell's equally substantial *Philosophy of Rhetoric*.

That said, Hume would make one enduring contribution to what we now call aesthetics, in the form of an essay entitled 'Of the Standard of Taste', first published in 1757. Here he addressed a question that naturally arose from his acceptance of Hutcheson's view that judgements of value are a function of sentiment, not reason. If that is the case, is the consequence that, as the saying goes, there is no arguing about matters of taste? That might be a matter of common sense, but, Hume observed, it contradicts another piece of common sense, which is that there would be something completely absurd in maintaining that, for example, there is no difference between the achievement of, say, Milton and some completely obscure poet whom no one has ever taken seriously. Extreme subjectivism was no more appropriate in criticism than it was in morals. The task Hume set himself in 'Of the Standard of Taste' was how to combine the existence of 'general rules of art', sufficient to distinguish between the good and the bad, with a commitment to aesthetic sentimentalism. His suggestion was that we understand the rules of art to have their source in the cultivated sensibility of experienced critics. The 'true standard of taste and beauty', Hume argued, is '[s]trong sense, united to delicate sentiment, improved by practice, perfected by comparison, and cleared of all prejudice' (*EMPL* 241).

The History of England would provide Hume with the opportunity to display his own sense of taste and beauty—and to reveal further how, despite his extraordinary adventurousness of mind, he was in some ways marked by the assumptions and prejudices of his age. It seems remarkable now, for example, that in his survey of the artistic achievements of the reign of James I, he should focus on the 'many irregularities, and even absurdities' in Shakespeare's plays. Shakespeare and Ben Jonson 'were equally deficient in taste and elegance', and '[t]he great glory of literature in this island, during the reign of James, was lord Bacon' (*HE* v 151, 153). *Paradise Lost* was Milton's 'capital performance', Hume accepted, but 'there are very long passages, amounting to near a third of the work, almost wholly destitute of harmony and elegance, nay, of all vigour of imagination' (*HE* vi 151). Of all the writers of the Restoration period, 'Sir William Temple is almost the only one, that kept himself altogether unpolluted by that inundation of vice and licentiousness, which overwhelmed the nation' (*HE* vi 544).

Of essay writing

Sometime in the early 1740s Hume decided that the systematic science of man undertaken in *A Treatise of Human Nature* was misconceived. He had had very high hopes for the first volumes of the *Treatise*, and was disappointed by the reception they met with. They were not completely ignored, but they did not effect the philosophical revolution that he had imagined they would. A long and demanding book like the *Treatise*, Hume now thought, was not suitable to the literary culture of the age. While he was working on Book Three of the *Treatise*, Hume had written a number of essays, apparently with a view to starting an Edinburgh-based magazine modelled on *The Spectator*, the enormously influential paper published daily by Joseph Addison and Richard Steele between March 1711 and December 1712. Nothing came of that plan. Instead Hume published two self-standing volumes of moral and political essays in 1741 and 1742.

The essay form promised a means of combining philosophical ingenuity and innovation with a language and argumentative style suited, as the *Treatise* apparently was not, to the expectations and capacities of the reading public. Hume's first collection of essays began with an essay about the writing of essays. There he portrayed himself as 'a Kind of Resident or Ambassador from the Dominions of Learning to those of Conversation' (*EMPL* 535). He expressed regret that learning had up until recently been confined to universities and monasteries. This, he claimed, had had a bad influence both on taste and on the conversation of the polite world. For what could there be to write and talk about without knowledge of history, poetry, politics, and philosophy? The result was bound to be literature that was little more than gossip—or literature that strained for dramatic effect for its own sake. At the same time, learning, by locking itself away from the world, had degenerated into pedantry and stylistic barbarousness. The essayist would remedy these two problems simultaneously, by teaching learning to be polite and conversable, and by insinuating matters of interest and importance into drawing rooms and clubs.

Hume's way of expressing his ambitions as an essayist owed a great deal to Addison. 'Mr Spectator', the character invented by

Addison to serve as his own mouthpiece, had declared that he wanted it to be said of him that he had 'brought philosophy out of closets and libraries, schools and colleges, to dwell in clubs and assemblies, at tea-tables and coffee-houses'. Like Addison, Hume conceived of the essay as a means of addressing a specific readership. The very rich were 'too much immers'd in Pleasure'; the very poor were 'too much occupy'd in providing for the Necessities of Life, to hearken to the calm Voice of Reason' (*EMPL* 546). Those who were situated in between great wealth and extreme poverty, in 'the Middle Station of Life', stood to gain most from what the essayist had to offer. They had need of all the virtues, those of industry and integrity as well as those of humanity and affability, and had a better chance than either the great or the humble of acquiring both wisdom and practical ability. The essayist spoke to those in the middle station as an equal, and encouraged them to recognize their situation as the happiest of all, particularly insofar as they were the best placed to know the pleasures of friendship. The poor were too often prevented by their poverty from doing the good services out of which friendships are made; while the rich had always to worry that they were esteemed only for their wealth.

In an essay entitled 'Of Avarice' Hume addressed a vice to which, perhaps, those in the middle station in life were especially liable. He noted that while the obsession with acquiring money for its own sake had always been condemned by moralists and philosophers, it was hard to find a single example of anyone having been cured of it. Hume offered the reader not a cure for avarice, but rather an ingenious explanation of its cause. It is usually found in old men, or in men 'of cold tempers', because it is impossible for the human mind to lack passion entirely, and this is the passion that best suited the state of those in whom all other concerns have died away to nothing. Why is it that such a cold and spiritless passion is so often taken to extremes? Hume's answer was that this is because the coldness of the avaricious man makes him insensible to ordinary concerns for reputation, friendship, and pleasure, so that his passion is not moderated, as passions normally are, by awareness of how he stands in the eyes of others. There is nothing to be done about avarice but to laugh at it. Hume was 'more apt to approve of those, who attack it with wit and humour, than of those who treat it in a serious manner' (*EMPL* 571). He ended the essay with a fable of his own invention, intended to do no more than add to the already copious stock of witty jokes at the miser's expense.

Just as important to Hume as it had been to Addison was the devising of a literary style that would appeal to women as well as men. Mr Spectator had observed that women 'compose half the world, and are by the just complaisance and gallantry of our nation the more powerful part of our people'. Likewise, Hume described women as 'the Sovereigns of the Empire of Conversation', and declared that they were 'much better Judges of all polite Writing than Men of the same Degree of Understanding' (*EMPL* 535, 536). In an essay 'Of the Study of History' Hume concerned himself with recommending history to women 'as an occupation, of all others, the best suited both to their sex and education, much more instructive than their ordinary books of amusement, and more entertaining than those serious compositions, which are usually to be found in their closets' (*EMPL* 563). History, in other words, was better for women than either novels or sermons and manuals of religious devotion. In another essay, 'Of Love and Marriage', Hume addressed matters with which women were usually supposed to be naturally more concerned than men, and took it upon himself to explain to his female readership why men complained about the married state as often as they did.

It would be wrong, however, to conclude that in his essays Hume did no more than thoughtlessly reinforce the sexist prejudices of his time. It is true that he was no radical when it came to relations between men and women. In his discussion of chastity in Book Three of the *Treatise*, Hume failed to challenge the assumption that it was more important for women than for men to be restrained in their indulgence of the appetite for sexual pleasure. On the other hand, in classifying chastity and modesty as artificial virtues, he went some way towards demystifying them. It was 'obvious', Hume claimed, that there is no 'foundation in nature' for the restrictions imposed by society upon the speech, dress, and behaviour of women. The only question worth discussing was how the idea of the need for such restrictions arises 'from education, from the voluntary conventions of men, and from the interest of society' (*T* 570). And in the explanation he offered of why sexual continence is valued more in women than in men, and of why the habits associated with such continence continue to be valued in women even after they have passed child-bearing age, Hume made it obvious that there was no need to appeal either to religion or to some kind of intrinsic authority possessed by husbands and fathers over wives and daughters. Instead, all that needed to be taken into account was the fact that, while a father was expected to pay for the upbringing and education of his children, trivial facts of biology meant that only a woman's chastity guaranteed that the children he was financially responsible for really were his own.

Similarly, when, in an essay 'Of Polygamy and Divorces', Hume argued in favour of monogamy and against voluntary divorce, he did so in a manner intended to highlight the fact that what he was arguing for was a set of conventions, not a matter of natural law. In other times and places, both polygamy and divorce had been permitted. But there was much to be said for 'our present European practice with regard to marriage' (*EMPL* 190). Wives were treated better by their husbands where one man was matched with one woman. Where divorce was not permitted, children were spared the fate of being committed to the care of an indifferent or even hostile stepmother. It was easier for love between man and woman to develop into the calm and sedate affection of friendship, and the permanence of the union of the interests of husband and wife prevented each from having reasons

ESSAYS,

MORAL

AND

POLITICAL.

By DAVID HUME, Efq;

The THIRD EDITION, Corrected, with Additions,

LONDON:

Printed for A. MILLAR, over againft *Catharine Street*
in the *Strand*; and A. KINCAID in *Edinburgh*.

M.DCC.XLVIII.

3. The title-page of the 1748 edition of *Essays Moral and Political*.
This was the first of Hume's works not published anonymously.

to be suspicious of the other. The argument of the essay served to make intelligible what might otherwise have seemed to be a wholly arbitrary imposition.

As Hume saw it, the essay was above all a vehicle of moderation. The characteristic posture of the essayist was that of someone seeking to navigate a passage between opposites, so as to produce consensus and harmony where before there had been disagreement and conflict. The essay brought together the worlds of learning and of polite conversation. It brought together the concerns and manners of men and of women. And it allowed Hume to present his ideas as sensible compromises that showed the way beyond entrenched and poorly motivated philosophical extremes. In one of his earliest essays, 'Of Moral Prejudices', he pointed to the middle ground between those who cynically made fun of the very ideas of friendship, honour, and patriotism, and those who thought human beings capable of perfecting themselves through the transcendence of the concerns of everyday life. The essay form was a way of reframing, not abandoning, Hume's search for an understanding of the human condition that was answerable to the truth of our experience of ourselves (Figure 3).

Anatomical painting, painterly anatomy

With the turn to the essay came a change of mind on Hume's part about how he might approach the 'moral subjects' that remained his principal concern. While he was finishing Book Three of the *Treatise* he had a correspondence with Hutcheson, in the course of which Hutcheson complained about the overly austere and anatomical tone of Hume's prose. There was lacking, in Hume's paraphrase of Hutcheson's objection, 'a certain Warmth in the Cause of Virtue' (*LDH* i 32). Hume replied that this was an inevitable shortcoming of the kind of book that he was writing, but that, even so, he would see what he could do 'to make the Moralist & the Metaphysician agree a little better' (*LDH* i 33). To this end, he added a rather cursory final paragraph to Book Three indicating 'the *happiness*, as well as…the *dignity* of virtue' (*T* 620). In the years that followed, he seems to have decided that more could be done towards making anatomy compatible with the practical concerns of the moralizing painter. Here was another opposition that the essay form could help to overcome.

Hume's understanding of how anatomy and painting might agree is, however, not easy to characterize. For, as he intimated in the essay 'Of Avarice', moral improvement was not straightforwardly his goal. He did not seek to instruct his readers how they could be more perfect than they ordinarily were. The account of human nature given in Books One and Two of the *Treatise*, with its redescription of reason as a habit-driven operation of the associative imagination, made it impossible for Hume to believe that philosophy, in its traditional guise as an appeal to a distinctively human capacity for rational autonomy, might be able to increase the virtue and happiness of human beings. Of course it was true that there were a few people who enjoyed doing philosophy, for whom, indeed, philosophy was an essential part of a life worth living. But it would be absurd to pretend that this was true of humankind as such.

In the essay 'Of Moral Prejudices' Hume identified the Stoics as a school of philosophers especially given to assuming that the cultivation of rationality could improve—even perfect—the human condition. As we saw in Chapter 1, Hume had biographical reasons to be sceptical of Stoicism's claims for itself. He broadened out his critique of philosophy's therapeutic ambitions in a group of essays on 'the sentiments of sects, that naturally form themselves in the world, and entertain ideas of human life and happiness' (*EMPL* 138). In these essays Hume impersonates, in turn, the Epicurean, the Stoic, the Platonist, and the Sceptic. Writing in the first person, he summarizes the views of the first three of these schools of thought as to how happiness was to be achieved. The Epicurean makes the case for retreat from the world and the cultivation of the pleasures of friendship and conversation.

The Stoic speaks up for the active pursuit of virtue for its own sake. The Platonist advocates contemplation of the perfection of the divine mind. The Sceptic, in contrast, doubts whether happiness lies in any one particular approach to life. Philosophers in general are too given to ignoring 'the vast variety of inclinations and pursuits among our species; where each man seems fully satisfied with his own course of life, and would esteem it the greatest unhappiness to be confined to that of his neighbour' (*EMPL* 160). Philosophy can offer no medicine for every human mind. The apparent worth of each and every object in life is determined by the passions, and there is little that anyone can do about the passions that happen to predominate in their character.

It is reasonable to suppose that in 'The Sceptic', Hume spoke for himself. He consistently refused to set himself up as a teacher of how life ought to be lived. Instead, what he offered readers was something like a mirror in which they might see themselves as they really were, and so gain a realistic understanding of their capacities. In an essay 'Of the Dignity or Meanness of Human Nature' he rejected both the views of those who exaggerate human potential, by representing man as having been made in the image of God, and the views of those who reduce man to the status of an animal superior to other animals only in his vanity. Where, in the *Treatise*, he had himself insisted on comparisons between man and animal, now he worried about the consequences of depreciating the human species. He was, he wrote, 'of opinion, that the sentiments of those, who are inclined to think favourably of mankind, are more advantageous to virtue, than the contrary principles, which give us a mean opinion of our nature' (*EMPL* 81). This did not mean that he was prepared to go along with those who portrayed human beings as demigods, whose faculties of reason and will were so many signs of man's heavenly origins. What was needed in order to gain an accurate understanding of our capacities was for us to give up constantly comparing ourselves with God on the one hand and with the animals on the other, and to focus attention on human nature by itself, so as to gain a clearer appreciation of the character of the motives that shape our lives.

This, of course, had been precisely Hume's concern in Book Two of the *Treatise*, but there, maintaining the rigorous objectivity of the anatomist, he had refrained from any evaluation of human nature as such. He had not addressed the question, answered in one way by Mandeville and in a diametrically opposite way by Hutcheson, of the extent of human selfishness. Was it true that, really, there was no such thing as friendship or public spirit? In 'Of the Dignity or Meanness of Human Nature' Hume argued that those who believed this had been led astray, by the fact that acts of virtue or friendship are pleasurable, and by the fact that such acts help to satisfy our perennial desire for praise. It was wrong to infer fundamental selfishness from these facts, first because virtue produces pleasure, and does not arise from it; and secondly because, as Hume put it, '[t]o love the glory of virtuous deeds is a sure proof of the love of virtue' (*EMPL* 86). Negative, pessimistic estimations of human nature had the effect of discouraging people from exercising their natural tendencies to virtue, by making them believe that it is impossible for them to be what, in fact, they would find pleasure in being. The anatomy of human nature could serve a practical purpose by ridding people of misconceptions of themselves and their abilities. It would show that human beings were fitted by nature with dispositions to both their own happiness and the good of society at large.

This was as far as Hume would go towards a philosophy of improvement and edification. In need of a position in society, in 1744 he allowed his name to be put forward for the professorship of moral philosophy at the University of Edinburgh, but when he failed to get the job, he was not very disappointed. It is hard to imagine him doing what professors of moral philosophy were expected to do—which was to teach boys in their early teens their duties as fathers, husbands, citizens, and Christians. After a brief period as a tutor to the mentally unstable Marquess of Annandale,

Hume spent almost two years with the British army as secretary to General James St Clair. Then he returned to the family home in Chirnside, and in an extraordinary burst of intellectual energy wrote a number of major works, including a new book of moral philosophy. Initially conceived of as a series of self-standing but interconnected essays, it was published in 1751 as *An Enquiry into the Principles of Morals*.

The morality of common life

In 1746, while taking part in an abortive British attack on the French town of L'Orient, Hume witnessed the aftermath of a suicide attempt on the part of an army officer desperate not to have his honour tarnished by being sent home on account of nothing more serious than exhaustion and hunger. As the law required, Hume called for a surgeon, but the officer soon died from his self-inflicted wounds. 'Never a man exprest a more steady Contempt of Life', Hume wrote in a letter, 'nor more determind philosophical Principles, suitable to his Exit' (*LDH* i 97). Perhaps as a result of this experience, Hume later wrote (but never published) an essay on suicide, in which he argued that taking one's own life is not necessarily a transgression of one's duties either to God, to our neighbour, or to ourselves. Suicide 'may be free from every imputation of guilt or blame'—'according to the sentiments of all the antient philosophers' (*EMPL* 580). The absolute injunction against it ran counter to natural feeling, and was a prime example of how religious superstition violated ordinary moral common sense. Hume's rewriting of his moral philosophy was not motivated solely by a desire to make it easier to read. To a significant extent, it was informed by a vivid sense that there were ways in which Christian moral culture ran counter to the moral sentiments, with the result that people lived unhappier lives than they needed to.

The fundamental problem with the ethical theory of Christian modernity, Hume thought, was its obsession with the idea that some actions deserve to be called good *in themselves*, regardless of what their consequences turn out to be. Not giving in to the temptation to commit suicide was supposed to be morally admirable, even if the life that was thereby preserved was a miserable one. Refraining from 'self-murder' and staying at one's post in life was, simply, a matter of duty, and doing one's duty was intrinsically praiseworthy, just because it was one's duty—which meant, just because it was what God required of one. Hume's view was that this entire line of thought was an alien imposition upon natural moral feeling. It was not an exclusively modern, Christian line of thought. The Stoics accepted the permissibility of suicide, but they, too, had written in praise of the good in itself, what was really good even if it so happened that no one acknowledged it to be good. As Hume saw it, however, it was always appropriate to be suspicious of the moral hero who placed himself at odds with the common sense of his time and place. Vanity all too often explained an ostentatious concern for duty for duty's sake, regardless of the consequences. Commonsensical moral thought, by contrast, was able to justify itself to itself, precisely because it dwelled upon the obvious benefits and harms of courses of action. The plain utility of virtue was the principal theme of *An Enquiry concerning the Principles of Morals*.

Usefulness was obvious in the case of 'social virtues' such as benevolence and justice. In fact it was so obvious that there was every reason to conclude that these virtues were valued solely on account of their utility. If human circumstances were to change so much that rules of justice were no longer useful, abiding by those rules would no longer properly be regarded as virtuous. In the *Treatise* Hume had used the utility of conventions regarding property as part of his argument that justice is an artificial, not a natural, virtue. The fact that such conventions are essential to human society made it plausible that they had been invented to serve that purpose. There was no need to postulate an innate disposition to attach moral significance to them. Now, though, Hume was no longer interested in pointing to the artificiality of justice. In a footnote to an appendix, he dismissed the whole issue as a 'merely verbal' dispute (*E* 308).

In answer to the question of why the utility of an action or practice prompts us to call it morally good, Hume postulated a principle of 'humanity' that naturally interests us in the well-being of others. 'It appears', he wrote, 'that a tendency to public good, and to the promoting of peace, harmony, and order in society, does always, by affecting the benevolent principles in our frame, engage us on the side of the social virtues' (*E* 231). The same principle explained moral approval of virtues useful to their possessor rather than to society at large, such as good sense, enterprise, frugality, temperance, and perseverance. 'Humanity' was perhaps explicable in terms of the faculty of sympathy described in the *Treatise*, but the details of its operation were another thing not relevant to Hume's present purposes. It was the fact of the existence of humanity that mattered. It meant that there was no need to suppose that human beings are motivated only by self-interest. To take human nature to be fundamentally selfish made it natural to look to considerations of duty for duty's sake, cutting against the grain of inclination, as the basis of moral judgement and action. But, as Hume had argued in the essay 'Of the Dignity or Meanness of Human Nature', the selfish theory was not a view of human nature supported by observation and experience.

Hume acknowledged that an emphasis on the utility of virtue led to a blurring of the usual distinction between distinctively moral character traits and bodily and mental endowments, which were more a matter of luck than of choice and effort. For just as good sense, enterprise, and frugality are useful to their possessor, so also are beauty, bodily strength and dexterity, and hereditary wealth. Both kinds of quality are praised because they are useful, and this seemed to undermine the basis for supposing that there is a significant moral difference between them. Many estimable traits, attributes, and abilities are also valued on account of what Hume termed their 'agreeableness', either to ourselves, or to others (or to both). In addition to its good effects, there is, for example, something immediately pleasing about benevolence, in 'the very softness and tenderness of sentiment, its engaging endearments, its fond expressions, its delicate attentions, and all that flow of mutual confidence and regard, which enters into a warm attachment of love and friendship' (*E* 257). But there is the same immediate appeal to good humour, wit, and even cleanliness.

To acknowledge these facts was, obviously enough, to downgrade the moral significance of will and choice. The idea that the sphere of moral goodness is limited to the sphere of freedom and responsibility was, Hume thought, another peculiarly modern and Christian idea. It was at odds with the sentiments both of 'the antient philosophers' and of everyday life. The same could be said of the idea that there was something morally admirable in 'monkish virtues' such as '[c]elibacy, fasting, penance, mortification, self-denial, humility, silence, [and] solitude' (*E* 270). There is nothing either useful or agreeable to such practices. On the contrary, they serve only to stupefy the understanding and to harden the heart, to corrupt the imagination and to sour the temper. They could, then, be transferred to the catalogue of vices, not virtues.

Plenty of Hume's moderately religious friends and contemporaries would have agreed about the pointlessness of celibacy and fasting. Yet they found it impossible to accept that there was no more to morality than the useful and the agreeable. Hume would be widely criticized for omitting the voluntary and the dutiful from his analysis of personal merit, even by Adam Smith, who in many ways was deeply influenced by Hume's ideas. Humanity, Smith remarked, 'is the virtue of a woman'. 'The most humane actions,' he continued, 'require no self-denial, no self-command, no great exertion of the sense of propriety'. Hume's point, however, was precisely that morality does not need to be regarded as a matter of self-denial and self-command and exertion. He meant to

4. Portrait in oils of Hume by Allan Ramsay, 1755.

represent virtue as something engaging, easy, and familiar. Virtue's sole purpose 'is to make her votaries and all mankind, during every instant of their existence, if possible, cheerful and happy; nor does she ever willingly part with any pleasure but in the hopes of ample compensation in some other period of their lives' (*E* 279). The virtuous life is the life that human beings naturally want to live. The happiness that virtue brings is possible here and now. It does not require divine grace, nor any other kind of radical reform of the self.

The *Enquiry concerning the Principles of Morals* was intended to empower and inspire self-confidence in its readers. It showed them what they were really like. Contrary to what they were told by ministers and moralists, they were not selfish beings who needed ideas of duty in order to overcome their natural inclinations. There was nothing wrong with their natural inclinations. They could trust their sentiments as guides to life. More than once Hume declared that the *Enquiry* was his favourite among his books, and he did so perhaps because it was where he made it clearest that his commitment to analysis and 'anatomy', evident here in his uncovering of the ubiquity in the moral life of the useful and the agreeable, was not at odds with the ordinary commitments of everyday life. For, just like everything else, philosophy itself was good only insofar as it was useful, and, ideally, agreeable as well.

Moral progress

Hume was not blind to the fact that, just as different nations had different characters, different societies had different moral codes. In a fictional dialogue published with the *Enquiry*, he compared the morals of ancient Athens with those of modern France. The Athenian man of merit, given to pederasty, able to marry his half-sister, and in the habit of leaving unwanted children outside to die, 'might, in this age, be held in horror and execration'; while the French man of merit, unconcerned about his wife's adultery, servile in the face of tyranny, and disposed to fight to the death over trivial points of honour, 'might, with the Athenians, be an object of the highest contempt, even ridicule' (*E* 333). These were, though, merely different ways in which the same fundamental moral principles expressed themselves. All of the qualities and practices extolled by both the Athenians and the French were valued on account of their being useful or agreeable, to oneself or to others. As one of the speakers in the dialogue expresses the point, '[t]he Rhine flows north, and the Rhone south; yet both spring from the *same* mountain, and are also actuated in their opposite directions, by the *same* principle of gravity' (*E* 333).

Comparison of the modern world with the ancient was an 18th-century obsession, and it was common to think that in respect of moral culture, at least, the modern world was inferior to the ancient. It was common, moreover, to suspect that the modern world was inferior even to the ages of darkness and violence that had followed the decline and fall of Rome. Then at least, and as in the ancient world, men had valued liberty and independence above all things, and had been willing to devote themselves wholly to service to the nation. Now, by contrast, men had been made selfish and soft by the fruits of manufacturing and commerce, and were more concerned about their private lives than about the good of the community at large. One of the most striking aspects of Hume's moral thought is his unwillingness to buy into this narrative of moral decline. He was convinced that, on the contrary, there were significant respects in which the modern world of commerce was not just different, but also morally superior to the ancient. Hume was as interested in ancient Greece and Rome as any of his contemporaries, but he was no nostalgist. He was confident that, far from being a source of corruption, commerce and a thriving market for luxury goods went along with the improvement, not only of standards of living, but of morals as well.

There were, of course, some respects in which the ancient world was indeed morally superior to the modern. Its attitude to suicide was one salient example. The moral philosophy of Cicero, in particular, was more wholesome than that of popular Christian manuals of ethics such as Richard Allestree's *The Whole Duty of Man*. In many respects, Hume thought, Christianity had been a disaster for the moral culture of Europe. But the wounds it had inflicted had not been fatal. Ignoring the Christian religion's own

condemnations of worldly concerns, modern European nations
had devoted themselves to the pursuit of riches, and as they had
done so they had discovered, as Hume put it in an essay 'Of
Refinement in the Arts', that '*industry, knowledge,* and *humanity,*
are linked together by an indissoluble chain, and are found...to
be peculiar to the more polished, and, what are commonly
denominated, the more luxurious ages' (*EMPL* 271). A sign of the
superiority of the modern world was the fact that it was—so
Hume found reason to believe—considerably more populous than
the ancient. '[I]f every thing else be equal', he claimed, 'it seems
natural to expect, that, wherever there are most happiness and
virtue, and the wisest institutions, there will also be most people'
(*EMPL* 382).

It was not the case, however, that Hume was blind to the
persistence of widespread human unhappiness and suffering. He
may not have acknowledged the evils of slavery in its modern
form, but his writings provide ample testimony to a conviction
that, regardless of the ways in which things were improving in the
age of commerce, it remained true that the pains of life were
usually greater than the pleasures, in both number and intensity.
Hume pointed this out when discussing the question of how the
existence of evil, natural as well as moral, could be compatible
with the supposition of a benevolent God. In an early manuscript
fragment, he declared that he was 'apt to regard human life as a
scene of misery, according to the sentiments of the greatest
sages as well as of the generality of mankind, from the beginning
of the world to this day'. 'Victuals, wine, a fiddle, a warm bed, a
coffee-house conversation', he added, 'make a pitiful figure, when
compared with racks, gravels, infamy, solitude, and dungeons.'
Hume had no time at all for the Christian response that, when
seen in the larger context of the workings of providence, natural
and moral evils were revealed to be a means of producing
more good than otherwise would have been possible. There
was just no evidence, he retorted, for the hypothesis of a
providential scheme.

Nor was there evidence that such progress as had taken place in the modern world was bound to continue. In December 1750, just as Hume was finishing work on *An Enquiry concerning the Principles of Morals*, the young Anne-Robert-Jacques Turgot gave a lecture in Paris entitled 'A Philosophical Review of the Successive Advances of the Human Mind'. It presented a picture of the human race as slowly but endlessly marching towards greater and greater perfection. Hume had no such confidence. Nothing guaranteed that the current age of improvement would not be followed by decay and decline. Human beings remained permanently liable to inflict great harms upon themselves and upon others, through factionalism in politics, and fanaticism in religion.

Chapter 3
Politics

Politics, Hume wrote in the *Treatise*, 'consider[s] men as united in society, and dependent on each other' (*T* xix). In other words, politics considers men as living under government. For, unlike animals, human beings need government to keep them united in all but the smallest societies, and to make them accept their mutual dependence. Part of politics, for Hume, was an understanding of each individual's obligation to the government he or she lives under. It provided an account of that obligation's source, and also of its limits. This was a general question about political life as such. Hume was sceptical, though, about how much there was to say about political society in the abstract. 'I am apt…to entertain a suspicion', he confessed, 'that the world is still too young to fix many general truths in politics, which will remain true to the latest posterity' (*EMPL* 87). In the essays which he published in the early 1740s he focused mostly on the party divide that was a peculiar feature of the British political culture of the time. In a new collection of essays published in 1752 he considered what he took to be the distinctively modern political question of how government should act with respect to international trade. He spent the rest of the 1750s writing a study of the origins of Britain's unique form of political liberty, in the guise of a history of England 'from the Invasion of Julius Caesar to the Revolution in 1688'.

Political obligation

Hume included allegiance among the 'artificial' virtues sharply distinguished, in Book Three of the *Treatise*, from those 'natural' virtues, like benevolence, charity, and generosity, which we approve of because each and every instance of them plainly has a tendency to the good of mankind. It might well not be obvious why it is a matter of moral obligation to obey the laws laid down by those in power. That obligation, after all, derives not from the moral character of the laws themselves, but rather from the simple fact that they are made by those who claim authority to compel us to obey. And no human being, it would seem, possesses by nature special attributes that make it morally compulsory to do as they command. That this individual, or that family, has the right to command allegiance must ultimately always be a matter of convention, even if the origins of the convention are ancient and forgotten. In his rejection of the idea of natural political authority, Hume agreed with Hobbes and Locke, and disagreed with those who believed that a king's right to command could be derived directly from the will of God.

On the other hand, Hume found it impossible to accept the accounts given by Hobbes and Locke of the construction of political power. Those accounts locate the source of an individual's duty of allegiance in a voluntary and conscious act of consent. This, Hume argued, was implausible for at least two reasons. The first was that almost no one in ordinary life is aware of having done or said something by means of which they could be said to have consented to the government they live under. The second was that, even if this problem could be overcome, perhaps by means of the notion of 'tacit' or 'implicit' consent, there appeared to be no way of explaining the obligation to obey in terms of a prior obligation to keep to the terms of a promissory agreement. For it is no more obvious why there is a moral obligation to keep promises than it is why there is a moral obligation to allegiance.

The former kind of obligation is no more natural than the latter. Both, in the end, have to be accounted for in terms of beneficial consequences of general adherence to a convention.

The idea that it is a moral duty to maintain allegiance derives, according to Hume, from the fact that 'the execution of justice, in the stability of possession, its translation by consent, and the performance of promises, is impossible, without submission to government' (*T* 546). For this reason, submission to government is plainly in our interests. In addition, our natural tendency to sympathize with those harmed by instances of injustice supplements self-interest with the sense that the obligation to obedience is *moral* as well as merely prudential. In this way belief in the authority of government develops automatically and involuntarily. Allegiance is, like so much of life on Hume's picture of human nature, a matter of unconsciously acquired habit. Also a matter of habit, Hume added, is acceptance of the particular form of government one happens to have been born under. To demonstrate their legitimacy, most regimes have nothing to appeal to other than the fact that they have been in power for a long time. Usually their power is the product of violence, not agreement. But in politics, according to Hume, origins do not matter. 'Nothing', he points out, 'causes any sentiment to have greater influence upon us than custom, or turns our imagination more strongly to any object' (*T* 556).

The role played by utility in the origin of the idea of a moral duty of allegiance enabled Hume to combine, on the one hand, a rejection of consent as the basis of political obligation with, on the other, an acceptance of the right of resistance that many (though not all) consent theorists had been keen to establish. For where government fails to ensure the execution of justice, where property and contracts are not protected, where there is disorder and fear instead of order and confidence, there is bound to be a loss of confidence in government, and, in the end, a dissolution of the opinion that the government must be obeyed. The regime in place will then, regardless of how long it has been in place, look as though it is doing more harm than good. It will be natural for there to be a feeling that it needs to be replaced by another. The idea that a regime has to be obeyed regardless, and that resistance is always and everywhere necessarily a crime, is obviously incompatible with the purposes which government was invented to serve.

Even so, Hume thought, it is very seldom that a people can be absolutely certain that the consequences of trying to effect a change of government will be better than putting up with the incompetence, or worse, of the current regime. Philosophy is not capable of defining precisely when the right of resistance should be exercised. It was true that the existence of such a right was especially clear in a mixed government such as England's, where each element of the constitution had the right to defend its powers and privileges against incursions on the part of the other elements. But that did not make it any easier to apply principle to practice. In a carefully oblique, and very brief, discussion of the implications of his treatment of the right of resistance for the so-called Glorious Revolution—'that famous *revolution*, which has had such a happy influence on our constitution, and has been attended with such mighty consequences' (*T* 563)—Hume insinuated that it had not been clear even in 1688 that resistance was justifiable.

The justification of the Revolution, Hume went on, lay in, precisely, its 'influence' and 'consequences'. The present Hanoverian regime was no different from most others in relying for its legitimacy on the passage of time. 'Time and custom give authority to all forms of government', Hume explained, 'and all successions of princes; and that power, which at first was founded only on injustice and violence, becomes in time legal and obligatory' (*T* 565). The mere suggestion that the transfer of the crown from James II to William III had been an instance of 'injustice and violence' was incendiary, but Hume would not be disposed to change his view even in the fraught conditions of the aftermath of the Jacobite rebellion of 1745. On the contrary, he then wrote new essays on political obligation expressly designed to highlight the baselessness of the crass triumphalism of those who had defeated Bonnie Prince Charlie.

In 'Of the Original Contract' Hume laid out what has since become the classic critique of consent theory. In 'Of the Protestant Succession' he balanced the case for the transfer of the crown to the (Protestant) House of Hanover against the case for its remaining with the (Catholic) House of Stuart, and found that, as things had stood in the run-up to 1714 and the accession of George I, the advantages of such a transfer had not obviously outweighed the disadvantages. What, forty years on, demonstrated the legitimacy of the Hanoverians was not high political principle, but simply the fact that the Hanoverians were the ones in power, and that things had gone reasonably well since they had taken over. Hume told a friend that he hoped he had 'examin'd this Question as coolly & impartially as if I were remov'd a thousand Years from the present Period' (*LDH* i 112).

The politics of moderation

The Revolution of 1688 put in place a constitution which settled—if not in the minds of Jacobites, then in the minds of the vast majority—the great constitutional disputes of the 17th century over royal prerogative and parliamentary privilege. It did not, however, end the vicious party disputes that had shaped British politics since the breakdown in the 1670s of the post-Civil War consensus. 'Tories' remained at loggerheads with 'Whigs', and tensions heightened as first George I and then George II looked to the Whig Sir Robert Walpole to conduct the business of government as Britain's first 'prime minister'. In the 1720s and 1730s an unstable coalition of Tories and disaffected Whigs positioned themselves as a 'patriotic' opposition to Walpolean 'corruption', and gave voice to their complaints in a journal,

The Craftsman, mostly written by the ex-Jacobite Henry St John, Lord Bolingbroke.

In his first collection of *Essays, Moral and Political*, published in 1741, Hume informed the reader that he had taken *The Craftsman* as his model as well as *The Spectator*. But what Hume in fact intended to do was apply the moderation and balance of the Addisonian essay to the contemporary political scene, in order to make it comprehensible why British politics took the form it did. This, again, was a kind of 'anatomy'. The goal was not to heal the party divide, but to understand it better, and so to stop both sides of the divide using complaints about factionalism for factional purposes.

There was, Hume thought, no point in pretending that in modern Britain party rivalry could be replaced by a patriotic politics of national unity. In a country with a mixed constitution, where the principal offices of government were divided between monarch and parliament, it was inevitable that there would be hostility between, on the one side, those who gave pre-eminence to the crown as the basis of authority and stability, and, on the other side, those who looked to parliament for the defence of rights and liberty. For how, exactly, the balance of power was to be settled in a mixed constitution was bound to be a matter of opinion. Some people would be disposed to trust the crown and fear the people, others would be disposed to trust the people and fear the crown. In the language of the time, there was bound to be a 'court' party and a 'country' party. The opposing principles of these two parties were, Hume argued, 'the genuine divisions in the British government' (*EMPL* 71).

The basis of party dispute was, then, disagreement between judgements of self-interest. There were those who took their interests to be best defended by the crown, and those who took their interests to be best defended by parliament. The problem in Britain was that this division had been complicated, and made especially dangerous, by disagreements about supposed matters of principle. The Tories combined support for the crown with belief in divine right and indefeasible succession which entailed that only one family, the Stuarts, had a right to the throne. The Whigs combined faith in parliament with belief in a right of resistance, which entailed that it was in the end for parliament to decide who had a right to the throne. 'Parties from *principle*', Hume declared, 'especially abstract speculative principle, are known only to modern times, and are, perhaps, the most extraordinary and unaccountable *phænomenon*, that has yet appeared in human affairs' (*EMPL* 60).

Religious differences intensified political differences. A party that stood for authority and order was bound to be the party of the established church, since, as Hume put it, '[l]iberty of thinking, and of expressing our thoughts, is always fatal to priestly power, and to those pious frauds, on which it is commonly founded' (*EMPL* 65–6). A party that stood for liberty and protection of the rights of the individual, by contrast, was bound to be favoured by religious dissenters, since they could hope that it might establish, if not universal freedom of religion, then at least some toleration of religious heterodoxy. Like all religious disagreements, this was a disagreement that had a tendency to turn violent. Refusal to extend the scope of toleration could be portrayed as monarchical tyranny. Dissenting criticism of the Church of England could be portrayed as seditious hostility to the monarchy itself. The case of modern Britain helped confirm Hume's suspicion that Christianity had an ability unique among religions to turn political disputes into excuses for oppression and persecution.

In the age of Walpole and Whig supremacy, British party politics had become 'unnatural', even 'monstrous' (*EMPL* 612). A traditionally 'country' party, associated with religious dissent, was in power; and a traditionally 'court' party, associated with the established church, was in opposition. Hume did not accept that this meant that old party labels had lost their meaning.

Bolingbroke's claim that now there was only a divide between those who believed in the value of the post-1688 constitution, and a corrupt clique of power-hungry Whigs, was a self-serving obfuscation of the political facts. The Tories had reinvented themselves as a party of liberty and the Revolution settlement, but remained committed above all to monarchical principles, which was ultimately what explained the animosity between them and the Hanoverian kings. They could not wholly accept a king put on the throne by parliament, and such a king was bound to be hostile to them. The Whigs had become the party of authority and the recipients of offices and pensions given by the crown, but, if forced to choose, they would choose liberty over allegiance to a particular royal family. It was for these reasons that the Church of England remained attached to the Tories, and Dissenters still connected themselves with the Whigs. Party politics was, then, at bottom, what it always had been, which meant that a return to the conflicts of the previous century was always possible. To understand this, Hume thought, was to understand how important it was that there be moderation on both sides of the party divide.

Hume hoped that such moderation would be fostered by a demonstration that there was a contradiction built into the extreme language each party used in its attacks on the other. Whigs claimed that no one but Walpole was capable of defending the Revolution settlement, while Tories claimed that, on the contrary, Walpole and his policies would destroy it. Both lines of argument, Hume pointed out, were incompatible with the veneration their exponents professed to feel for the constitution put in place after 1688. The constitution as both parties described it was not such as to be reliant on one man for its continued existence, and nor was it such that one man might do it fatal damage. The whole point of a good constitution, after all, was that it did not matter who occupied positions of power. A good constitution was, as the saying had it, a government of laws, not men. The rule of law was what distinguished a free system of government, the kind of government that both parties said they valued above all things, from absolutism.

This, however, was an argument that could itself become a source of irrational, and dangerous, animosity. Hume was well aware that, divided into factions though they were, the British—or rather, perhaps, the *English*—could come together in an arrogant, and uninformed, sense of their superiority over most of their fellow Europeans. British liberty was routinely trumpeted as a rebuke to despotism on the continent, and to French despotism in particular. But, Hume thought, overvaluation by the British of their constitution was as pernicious as undervaluation. Moderation required an appreciation of the fact that there were respects in which absolute states were superior to free ones. Hume made this point in a substantial essay 'Of the Rise and Progress of the Arts and Sciences', where he argued that while it was true that the origins of learning and culture lay in freedom, and while the sciences tended to flourish most in republics, it was in monarchies such as France that the arts were being brought to perfection.

The crucial fact here was that in modern Europe, absolute monarchies had become, as Hume put it, 'civilized'. Kings no longer sought to impose themselves into every aspect of government. Administration, including most importantly the administration of justice, had been allowed to become independent of the whims of a single man. This meant, Hume argued in an essay 'Of Civil Liberty', that it was no longer true that absolutism entailed despotism and the absence of liberty. Civilized monarchies, just as much as republics, could be called governments of laws, not men. 'They are found susceptible of order, method, and constancy, to a surprizing degree,' Hume rhapsodized. 'Property is there secure; industry encouraged; the arts flourish; and the prince lives secure among his subjects, like a father among his children' (*EMPL* 94). There was an international dimension to the moderation that Hume sought to instil in his readers. A sober, anatomical understanding of Britain's situation required a tempering of claims about the unique virtues of the country's constitution.

Political economy

In the essay 'Of Civil Liberty' Hume argued that republics such as the Netherlands and almost-republics such as Britain were doing well at international trade only because in pure monarchies like France commerce was still regarded as not the proper concern of a man of honour. That, however, was hardly likely to be a permanent barrier to French commercial success. Quite generally, Hume pointed out, trade had not been regarded as an affair of state until the 17th century. It was not until England and the Dutch Republic had, despite their modest size, achieved opulence, grandeur, and military success that kings and their ministers recognized the importance of an extensive commerce. Neither the political philosophers of the ancient world nor those of the Italian city states had had anything to say about how government should address itself to the questions of trade. What would soon become known as the science of political economy was still in its infancy. In a new series of essays largely written, like *An Enquiry concerning the Principles of Morals*, while he was at home in Chirnside between 1749 and 1751, Hume devoted himself to making the politics of commerce better understood. His goal in *Political Discourses* was not a systematic treatment such as would soon be laid out in Smith's *The Wealth of Nations*. Instead, he wanted to persuade his readers to re-examine their assumptions, and to get them thinking critically about what had become accepted as mere common sense.

Most fundamentally, Hume wanted his readers to reconsider the traditional idea that the wealth generated by commerce was inevitably a threat to a nation's moral health. There was a powerful current of political thought that held up the fierce independence of ancient Sparta and of the Roman republic as the essence of liberty, and that saw commerce, and especially the trade in luxury goods, as fatal to austere patriotic commitment to the good of the state over the good of the individual. As we saw in Chapter 2, Hume's contrary view was that an increase in national prosperity naturally went along with an improvement in manners and morals. This was one reason why it was wrong to see the history of the modern world as a story of decline. It was true that Spartan and Roman values had lost their appeal, but that did not mean that modern states must be weaker than their ancient ancestors. What the examples of the Dutch Republic and England showed was that in fact successful commerce made states stronger. Here was a new, distinctively modern understanding of liberty, in the form of the protection of property and the unrestricted expression of enterprise. The spirit of commerce was identical with the spirit of liberty so understood. Hume, Smith would remark, was the first writer on politics to have seen the tight connection between commerce, good government, and the liberty and security of the individual.

The question for politicians, then, was how they could help commerce have its naturally beneficial effect on the condition of the nation. Hume was sure that this question was being answered in the wrong way. It was understandable that people would assume that the proper goal of commerce was the accumulation of money, where money was another name for gold and silver. On this assumption, commerce was a kind of war between nations, and a sign that the war was being won was that money was flowing into one nation and out of the others. In other words, a 'positive' balance of trade was what mattered, and it would be achieved by making sure that the value of exports was always greater than the value of imports. An essential means of making as much money as possible from exports, moreover, was to keep wages low. It was understandable to think this way, Hume accepted, but it was also completely mistaken. Money was not what commerce was about. It was a means, not an end. It was no more than an instrument of exchange, not the wheel of trade, but, as Hume put it, 'the oil which renders the motions of the wheels more smooth and easy' (*EMPL* 281).

It was not obvious, Hume asserted in this essay, that it mattered how much money a country possessed. Prices would always adjust to the quantity of money, rising as it increased, falling as it decreased. It was not even straightforwardly the case that amassing money was advantageous to a state's dealings with other states. Money was useful in wars and negotiations, but it also had the effect of making a country's exports more expensive to other countries—and of making a poorer country's imports cheaper. Yet there clearly was some connection between money and national prosperity. Countries which had seen a significant addition to their holdings of gold and silver—as had many European countries since the discovery of the Americas—had seen rises in the standard of living. Countries where there was a shortage of gold and silver were, even if they had a flourishing population and copious food supply, incapable of asserting themselves on the international stage. Hume argued that the explanation lay in the effects of *increases* in the quantity of money. A rise in the quantity of money stimulated the economy regardless of the amount of the money in the economy to start with. It generated new wealth, which the state could tax and use to improve its international standing.

An increase in the money supply had these effects because of the way in which it stimulated industry and enterprise. There was a period between the arrival of new money and the eventual concomitant rise in prices when landowners and merchants and traders would put the money to work, borrowing from those who brought the money in, and trying to gain an advantage over their competitors by investing in new techniques and taking on additional labour. They would then find they had more disposable income, to reinvest, but also to spend on themselves and on their families. They would buy finer clothes and build bigger houses, which would in turn increase the prosperity of others. Eventually money would diffuse itself through the population and prices—of both commodities and labour—would increase to a point where the economy slowed down again. Before that happened, though, an efficient tax regime would ensure that the state enriched itself just as did the population at large. Most important to any country's economy, in other words, was the appetite and ability of its people to make use of increases in the money supply. The supposed effects of a scarcity of money were actually, as Hume put it, the 'collateral effects' of the manners and customs of a people not disposed to work to improve their standard of living.

It followed that what a government needed to do in its management of the national economy was above all to allow habits of industry and enterprise to have their usual effects. Government had a duty, of course, to protect property and enforce the rule of law. It also had a role to play in the coordination of effort necessary to large capital projects such as the construction of bridges and harbours. But mostly what government needed to do was to get out of the way, and allow landowners, manufacturers, and traders to conduct their businesses as they judged best—even if that meant the export of essential commodities such as wheat and wool, and the import of the products of commercial rivals. Tariffs and controls were, in general, unnecessary and counterproductive. Trade should be as free as possible, allowing for the occasional need for the protection of fledgling industries. Taxes should be levied in a way that would stimulate, not inhibit, economic activity.

Hume was encouraging a reconceptualization of the nature of national wealth. A country's prime resource was not its stock of money, but rather the energy and inventiveness of its people. At the same time, Hume sought to persuade his readers to rethink their understanding of international relations. The logic of trade was entirely different from that of the zero sum competition for territory and resources (especially gold and silver) in which European states had been engaged since the end of the 16th

5. **Drawing of Hume by Louis Carrogis, *c*.1764.**

century. There was a not a finite amount of wealth to be divided among the countries of the world. In order for a country to enrich itself by trade, it needed its neighbours to be able to afford to buy its products, and in order for them to be able to do that, they too needed to develop the arts and sciences of agriculture and manufacture. In an essay added in 1758, Hume declared that it was therefore 'not only as a man, but as a British subject' that he prayed for 'the flourishing commerce of Germany, Spain, Italy, and even France itself' (*EMPL* 331).

All European countries had taken on massive amounts of debt to pay for the wars in which the contest for new raw materials and markets was played out. Britain was no exception. Hume rejected arguments that a national debt was no cause for concern because it was, in effect, a debt which the nation owed to itself. There was always an international dimension to a country's indebtedness, regardless of the fact that its principal creditors were its own citizens. A crisis in Britain's external relations would be bound to tempt desperate politicians to raid and exhaust the funds put aside for debt repayment, with fatal consequences for its creditors and creditworthiness. Alternatively, the country might decide that it was no longer willing to take such risks, and that in future it would play no part in the preservation of a balance of power in Europe. It might prefer to see its neighbours oppressed and conquered—to the point where it itself lay at the mercy of the conqueror. Britain was taking on so much debt, Hume feared, that, in an unstable world, its choice would ultimately be between the 'natural' and 'violent' deaths of its public credit.

The history of British liberty

Hume published *Political Discourses* to international acclaim in 1752. It was, he later wrote, 'the only book of mine that was successful on the first publication'. The year before, he had finally left the family home and set up house in Edinburgh. Scotland's capital was at just this time seeing the first signs of the cultural and scientific developments that would soon give it a claim to be regarded as a significant contributor to the Europe-wide intellectual revolution that we now call the Enlightenment. A 'Philosophical Society' had been founded in 1749, Adam Smith was giving public lectures on recent developments in rhetoric and jurisprudence, and the city's literati were starting a new literary journal, *The Edinburgh Review*. A self-consciously 'moderate' party of ministers was beginning to make itself heard in the annual General Assembly of the Church of Scotland. Hume found a place at the heart of this ferment of activity as Librarian to Edinburgh's Faculty of Advocates. The job did not pay much, but it did give Hume easy access to a wide ranging and up-to-date collection of 30,000 books. It was the perfect position for someone whose next literary project was a new British history, beginning with the union of crowns in 1603 and ending with the Revolution of 1688. Hume had been thinking about writing a history for some time. Now he had the opportunity.

The History of Great Britain was published in two instalments, in 1754 and 1757. Hume then decided that in order to make full sense of what had happened in Britain in the 17th century, it was necessary to start with the reign of the House of Tudor. After all, it was with the Tudors that—so Hume wrote to a friend—modern history began: 'America was discovered: Commerce extended: The Arts cultivated: Printing invented: Religion reform'd: And all the Governments of Europe almost chang'd' (*LDH* i 249). The completion of the story, however, turned out to require that he take things all the way back to the Roman conquest. In this way what had begun as a history of Great Britain became a history of England alone—though, inevitably, relations with Scotland were a constant theme, along with relations with Ireland and France. Despite the fact that the pre-Tudor part of English history turned out to be 'a Work of infinite Labour & Study' (*LDH* i 321), it took only four years to make the journey all the way back from Elizabeth to the Roman invasion. Hume had finished his historical labour and study by 1762.

In the Stuart volumes of the *History* Hume presented his reader with a sceptical examination of the narratives constructed by both Whigs and Tories for use in the party political battles that the Revolution had failed to bring to an end. In the first instance this required a reopening of the question of who had been responsible for the Civil War, the execution of Charles I, and the Cromwellian tyranny of the 1650s. Whigs pinned the blame on the Stuart kings, and their ministers, for systematically violating the ancient privileges of people and parliament. Tories, by contrast, blamed successive Houses of Commons for failing to contain republican radicals, who, inspired by a Puritan hatred of the political and ecclesiastical establishment, refused to respect the equally ancient prerogatives of the crown and the Church. Hume sought to weave together key themes from both perspectives on the history of the first half of the 17th century. The Commons—egged on by religious extremists—had indeed continually put pressure on the established balance of power between king and parliament, as they had become aware of, and sought to exploit, a growing financial advantage over the crown. James I and then his son Charles had failed to understand the way the ground was shifting under their feet, and had exacerbated the tension by reasserting their right to prerogative powers that, in truth, they were no longer able to exert.

The ensuing disaster was the fault of both sides. It also failed to solve the underlying problem. Charles II and James II would continue to appeal to tradition and precedent in order to lay claim to rights—crucially, to an income from parliament sufficient to enable the crown to play its role as the executive arm of the state—which parliament was increasingly disposed not to recognize. This tempted each king to try to rule without parliament, something that was only possible, in fact, with the secret financial support of the king of France. Tension between king and commons (and lords) was further heightened, in the end fatally, by the Catholic sympathies of the later Stuarts. In 1688, when the openly Catholic James II announced the birth of a son and heir, parliament looked across the North Sea to William of Orange, the Protestant husband of James's Protestant half-sister Mary, to solve the problem once and for all. Henceforth England would have a monarch who could not help but recognize his, or her, fundamental dependence upon the good will of parliament.

Hume described England's journey towards 1688 in a carefully even-handed way. What doctrinaire Whigs represented as malevolent Stuart despotism, Hume portrayed as a series of mistakes on the part of men whose ignorance of political reality was as understandable as it was regrettable. Hume appeared, in fact, to go out of his way to bring out the virtues of the Stuart kings, along with the vices and absurdities of their enemies. Summing up at the end of the reign of Charles I, he opined that the king's 'virtues predominated extremely above his vices, or, more properly speaking, his imperfections: For scarce any of his faults rose to that pitch as to merit the appellation of vices' (*HE* v 542). James II was 'more unfortunate than criminal' (*HE* vi 520). Resistance and revolution in 1688, ultimately beneficial though it had turned out to be, was in no way comparable to the overthrow of a Nero or a Domitian. Oliver Cromwell, on the other hand, was a bigot and a hypocrite, a man whose religious fanaticism was never anything other than a mask for his overheated political ambition.

What Hume repeatedly emphasized was that the Stuarts could be excused their mistakes about the extent of their prerogative powers because the image they had had of English kingship had been a reality during the age that had gone before them. Contrary to cherished myth, Stuart tyranny had not been preceded by a golden age of liberty under Elizabeth. England under the Tudors had been just like modern-day Turkey—18th-century Europe's favourite example of 'Asiatic despotism'. Whig historians of Elizabeth's reign had 'been so extremely ignorant…as to extol her for a quality, which, of all others, she was the least possessed of: a tender regard for the constitution, and a concern for the liberties and privileges of her people' (*HE* iv 354). What was more, parliament, supposedly the voice of the spirit of English liberty, had consistently failed to challenge the idea that Tudor monarchs had of the extent of their authority. Elizabeth had been popular for so much of her long reign precisely because she ruled in perfect conformity with the opinion of the people at large.

Tudor power was in part a consequence of Henry VIII's break with Rome and the consequent combination of the roles of head of state and head of the Church. After the Reformation, religion was 'the capital point, on which depended all the political transactions of that age' (*HE* iv 176). Puritanism raised its head not long afterwards, and Hume was prepared to accept that, in an era of political absolutism, it was religious enthusiasts who kindled and preserved 'the precious spark of liberty' (*HE* iv 145–6). It was a mistake, however, to suppose there was any sense in which the Puritans articulated an intrinsically English thirst for freedom. The majority of the English still favoured 'Romish' ritual in church services, and Elizabeth's caution and compromise in religious matters was an important part of what made her so popular with her people.

Just as important as the consequences of the Reformation, on Hume's analysis, were the consequences of changes made by Henry VII to the feudal law of property. From this time onwards it was possible for the great landowners to mortgage and alienate their land, which simultaneously freed up capital for consumption of luxury goods, and gave an incentive to new, middle-ranking proprietors to increase the productivity of their farms. This was the moment when the breakdown of feudal aristocracy began, as the balance of power in the English constitution slowly began to shift away from the nobility and towards the House of Commons. Yet it would take 200 years for this massive alteration in the dynamics of English politics to work itself out. The immediate consequence was a power vacuum created as noble families became more interested in conspicuous consumption than in maintaining huge numbers of armed retainers. It was this vacuum that the Tudor monarchs quickly moved to fill, replacing a permanently unstable network of baronial rivalries with a much more autocratic, top-down system of national administration.

The Tudor period, then, saw the end of what had been a long and often violent struggle for domination between kings and barons. Whig historians wanted to find in the Middle Ages evidence of the resuscitation of supposedly ancient conceptions of the rights of the individual and of parliament, but Hume agreed with the Tory critics of this interpretation of key events such as Magna Carta and the first meetings of the House of Commons. There had been, he argued, no idea of individuals having rights independently of, and potentially against, the monarch. Freedoms were taken to be grants of the crown. The structure of parliament had undoubtedly changed during the reign of Henry III, when Henry invited knights from the shires and deputies from the boroughs to join his body of advisers, but this was merely a means whereby Henry sought to counter the power of the aristocracy. It was not a recognition of an age-old right of the people to be part of the legislative process. The king thought that this new power in the constitution would be more submissive than the barons; and the people thought that the king would, in return for their submission, protect them from the predations of their feudal superiors.

Hume accepted that the signing of the Magna Carta by John in 1215 was an epochal event. But this was so only when one considered its very long-term effects. At the time it marked no revolution in the standing of the individual in relation to the power of the crown. 'It only guarded', Hume claimed, 'and that merely by verbal clauses, against such tyrannical practices as are incompatible with civilized government, and, if they become very frequent, are incompatible with all government' (*HE* i 487). And it did very little to change how kings actually governed. Its clauses were routinely ignored by English monarchs until the end of the

17th century. It took that long, in other words, for the crown to accept that its freedoms, just as much as those of its subjects, were bound and defined by law. In its 13th-century context, moreover, Magna Carta was a victory for the barons, not for the people at large. It meant that they, and no longer the king, were 'really invested with the sovereignty of the kingdom' (*HE* i 447).

Magna Carta was a sign that the feudal system of law, imposed on England in the wake of the Norman conquest in 1066, was beginning to break down. Yet this process of dissolution could not, according to Hume, be understood as the reclamation of a freer and more 'balanced' form of government that had existed among the Anglo-Saxons. For one thing, the consequence of 1066 had been the complete obliteration of all previously existing legal forms. It really had been a *conquest*, and not, as Whigs liked to think, a temporary occlusion of an enduring tradition of common law. For another thing, there was little to admire when one looked back beyond the reign of William I. What some fondly called true English liberty was in fact mere anarchy. No middle ground was discernible between the tyrannical licentiousness of an ungovernable nobility and the demeaning slavery of their dependants. '[T]he great body of the people, in these ages', Hume observed, 'really enjoyed much less true liberty, than where the execution of the laws is the most severe, and where subjects are reduced to the strictest subordination and dependance on the civil magistrate' (*HE* i 168–9). It was, in other words, nonsense to claim, as Montesquieu did in *The Spirit of Laws*, that the origins of modern English freedom were to be found in the forests of a thousand years ago.

Having written and published his history of England backwards, beginning with the Stuarts and ending with the Middle Ages, Hume assembled a collected edition of all six volumes in 1762. Taken as a whole, the *History of England* combined a great deal of Tory critique of Whig myth-making with a larger, and fundamentally Whig, confidence in the benefits of the Revolution of 1688. The Revolution, Hume concluded, 'gave such an ascendant to popular principle, as has put the nature of the English constitution beyond all controversy'. 'And it may justly be affirmed', he added, 'without any danger of exaggeration, that we, in this island, have ever since enjoyed, if not the best system of government, at least the most entire system of liberty, that ever was known amongst mankind' (*HE* vi 531). At the same time, however, Hume undercut both Tory and Whig approaches to English history by depicting 1688 as the product of historical forces that had worked themselves out mostly regardless of personalities and policies. Where individuals and their decisions had been important, it had been because of consequences unintended and unforeseen. It was the adoption of this elevated, disengaged, *philosophical* perspective that gave Hume, as he put it in a letter, 'the impudence to pretend that I am of no party, and have no bias' (*LDH* i 185).

The overall political lesson that Hume offered his reader was that, far from restoring England's ancient constitution, the Revolution had put in place an entirely new balance of power between crown and parliament. Taken as a whole, English history was a story of a succession of different constitutions: the pre-Norman, the feudal, the Tudor, and the modern. 'The English constitution, like all others', Hume remarked, 'has been in a state of continual fluctuation' (*HE* iv 355). The *History of England*, then, could be seen as, paradoxically enough, an attempt on Hume's part to release British politics from the grip of history. Since the Civil War, history had been used as a political weapon. Hume's message was that, properly understood, it could serve the polemical purposes of neither party. In any age, Hume claimed at the end of the volume he wrote last, 'the only rule of government, which is intelligible or carries any authority with it, is the established practice of the age, and the maxims of administration, which are at that time prevalent, and universally assented to' (*HE* ii 525).

Solving the problem of style

Hume did not intend the *History of England* to be read only as an extended piece of political philosophy. He took seriously the task of recounting the history of the British from 'when Caesar...first cast his eye on their island' (*HE* i 6) to the Declaration of Right presented by parliament to William and Mary in February 1689. The *History* was meant to find a place among, while contrasting with, the many other histories of England written in the first half of the 18th century. It would be distinctive, Hume hoped, precisely insofar as it was *less* political—less partisan, more impartial—than history writing in English tended to be. Voltaire had noted that the English had yet to produce a history worthy of an international readership. The reason was the fact that '[o]ne half of the nation is always at variance with the other half'. '[T]he English have memorials of the several reigns', Voltaire decided, 'but no such thing as a history.' Montesquieu had come to the same conclusion, explaining this failure of the English in terms of the extreme form of liberty that prevailed among them. Such liberty was bound, Montesquieu thought, to produce faction, and faction was bound to produce factional history. Hume set out to prove that it was possible for an English—or rather British—historian to transcend party politics and write in a manner comparable to Machiavelli, Guicciardini, Sarpi, and, indeed, Voltaire himself.

Hume declared in a letter that 'My views of *things* are more conformable to Whig principles; my representations of *persons* to Tory prejudices' (*LDH* i 237). Impartiality was to be achieved not so much by adopting an entirely new perspective on the reigns of English kings and queens as by combining perspectives that were usually assumed to be incompatible. The overall argument was, as we have seen, a vindication of 1688, and so a vindication also of the moves made to limit royal power by successive parliaments in the 17th century. But at the same time, as we have also seen, Hume refused to follow Whig historians in condemning the Stuart kings as nothing but power-hungry tyrants. He wanted to show them to be human beings deserving, as all human beings must be in extreme circumstances, of sympathy and a measure of compassion. In his depiction of the execution of Charles I, for example, he is not afraid to echo some of the themes of royalist hagiography. During his final days, Hume's Charles is a model of dignity and self-control. He sleeps soundly despite the fact that work was being done round the clock on the scaffold outside his window. He forgives his enemies before the axe falls. And his death fully restores him to the favour of his people, so much so that on hearing of it '[w]omen are said to have cast forth the untimely fruit of their womb', while '[o]thers fell into convulsions, or sunk into such a melancholy as attended them to their grave' (*HE* v 541).

There is more, in other words, to Hume's *History* than philosophical detachment. In another letter he told a friend that 'The first Quality of an Historian is to be true & impartial; the next is to be interesting' (*LDH* i 210). Here 'interesting' means being such as to engage sympathy and sentiment. There are many places in the book where analytical precision gives way to what can only be called melodrama. 'No age, no sex, no condition was spared,' Hume writes in his description of the Irish rebellion of 1641. 'The wife weeping for her butchered husband, and embracing her helpless children, was pierced with them, and perished by the same stroke' (*HE* v 341). The punishments inflicted in the west of England after the failure of Monmouth's invasion in 1685 are itemized in the same gory detail, not excluding 'the wanton savage' Colonel Kirke's instruction that music be played to accompany the 'dancing' of those whose feet shook as they were hanged (*HE* vi 462). Another way of describing Hume's technique might be to say that he alternated the dispassionate observation of the philosopher with the emotional manipulation of the novelist.

6. Frontispiece to the 1770 edition of *The History of England*, from a drawing of Hume by John Donaldson.

The *History of England* (Figure 6) was intended to reach a maximally wide readership, among Tories as well as among Whigs, among women as well as among men, among Frenchmen (and other Europeans) as well as among the Scottish and English. Hume wanted, above all, to be readable. Another important means to that end was, simply, brevity. Long though it is, Hume's *History* is shorter than most others, and was not published in massive folio volumes that needed to be read on a desk or lectern. Most editions comprised eight small 'quarto' volumes. They were printed in large numbers. They sold at a relatively cheap price. And they made their author a wealthy man. Hume made more than £4,000 from the sale of the rights to the successive instalments of the *History*—perhaps £500,000 in the money of today.

Reasons for pessimism

Hume wrote the *History of England* at a time when he felt moderately optimistic about Britain's political prospects. The decisive defeat of the Jacobite army at Culloden in 1746 meant that the traumas of the previous century could be left behind. For a moment, at the end of the reign of George II, he allowed himself to hope that a new political era was about to start. In a new essay 'Of the Coalition of Parties', he welcomed the development of a kind of politics that 'affords the most agreeable prospect of future happiness, and ought to be carefully cherished and promoted by every lover of his country' (*EMPL* 494). A new king would be followed by new ministers, and by the fall of a government, led by the Whig William Pitt, that had involved Britain in what appeared to be an endless, and infinitely expensive, war with France over who would be dominant in America.

Pitt was indeed dismissed by the new king George III, but war continued until 1763. In a new edition of his *Essays* published a year after the Treaty of Paris, Hume made changes to his discussion of the national debt which suggested that his optimism had already deserted him. Indeed, as he contemplated the extent to which politicians had mortgaged future tax income in order to pay for the Seven Years War, Hume finally lost all confidence in the supposed benefits of British liberty. The cost of servicing the national debt would soon, he thought, be too great for any government. A choice would have to be made between the interests of the country's creditors and the interests of the country itself. The same choice would have to be made by other countries too, but Britain, Hume worried, was at a peculiar disadvantage. For Britain's creditors were, in large part, those who ran the country. They were members of the House of Commons and the House of Lords—or were closely connected with them. Parliament would therefore naturally resist any move to default on the national debt. In an absolutism like France, by contrast, it was possible in principle for the monarch to default regardless of the complaints of his creditors. When Hume looked to the future, he saw—mistakenly, of course—disaster for Britain, and triumph for its ancient enemy.

Hume's pessimism increased as the 1760s wore on. In 1768–9 he witnessed riots in London following the expulsion from the Commons of the dissident MP and journalist John Wilkes. Hume was appalled by what he saw as the government's pusillanimity in dealing with the mob. He told Turgot that the chaos provided decisive evidence against the idea that society was progressing towards perfection. England was, he thought, in the grip of political madness. The rioters had no grievances worthy of the name. They demanded liberty without having any understanding of what it meant, and, most dangerously of all, without awareness that liberty was an empty word without the protections offered by countervailing forces of authority. Hume wrote a new essay, 'Of the Origin of Government', to try to make this clear. The enfeeblement of the executive meant that the balance of power in Britain was shifting towards the mass of the people, and that, Hume had no doubt, was bound to be followed by the rise of a demagogic Caesar-figure who would trample on the principles of the constitution in the name of the brutish majority. Any move towards republicanism in a state as large as Britain, Hume told his nephew, 'can...produce only Anarchy, which is the immediate Forerunner of Despotism' (*LDH* ii 306).

News of first discontent and then open revolt in the American colonies confirmed Hume in his sense that the British form of government was falling apart. So incompetent were those in power that the loss of the empire was nothing other than what they deserved. It was also true, however, that it was 'in the Nature of things' that the union with America 'cannot long subsist' (*LDH* ii 237). America's growth in population and assertiveness meant that very soon the cost of keeping the colonies under the mother country's rule would be greater than the income generated by taxation of American trade. 'Nations, as well as Individuals,' Hume wrote to a friend, 'ha[ve] their different Ages, which challeng[e] a different Treatment' (*LDH* ii 288). The American colonies were no longer young and childlike, and nothing good would come of pretending otherwise. Rather than try to hang on to them at any cost, it would be in Britain's interests to let them go, and to trade with them on equal terms. This was what Hume meant when he said in a letter written in October 1775 that 'I am an American in my Principles, and wish we would let them alone to govern or misgovern themselves as they think proper' (*LDH* ii 303). Hume died soon after the Declaration of Independence, but, had he lived longer, would have been surprised neither by the British state's refusal to let America alone nor by its eventual defeat.

Chapter 4
Religion

Hume was extremely unusual among his contemporaries in having no emotional need for the promises and reassurances of the Christian religion. When it came to religion, even more so than when it came to politics, he was a bystander, with no positive commitments to defend. His letters make it clear that, looked at from this detached point of view, religion and religious people very often seemed absurd. He appears seldom to have refrained from making a joke at the expense of the pious and the sanctimonious whenever the opportunity presented itself. But at the same time Hume was fascinated by religion, and wrote a great deal about it. He examined the rational basis both of belief in the teachings revealed by sacred texts such as the Christian Gospels, and of belief in the 'natural' religion supposedly accessible to all human beings through the use of reason. The sceptical outcome of these investigations was supplemented—as, given religion's ubiquity, it needed to be—by an identification of the sources of religious belief in human nature. In many places in his writings, Hume considered the effects, usually deleterious, of religion on both morality and politics. It is not clear, though, what practical consequences, if any, Hume expected his writings on religion to have (Figure 7).

7. Portrait in oils of Hume by Allan Ramsay, 1766.

Religion in Hume's early writings

At first Hume intended to apply the scepticism of *A Treatise of
Human Nature* directly to questions in the philosophy of religion.
Then he changed his mind. In a letter sent in 1737 he described
himself as 'at present castrating my work, that is cutting off its
nobler parts; that is endeavouring it shall give as little offence as
possible' (*LDH* i 25). One of the parts in question was 'some

Reasonings concerning Miracles', a version of which was later included in *An Enquiry concerning Human Understanding.* It is possible that the manuscript fragment on evil described in Chapter 2 was also originally meant for inclusion in the *Treatise*. Religion is barely mentioned in the published text, but there are places where the religious implications of Hume's arguments would have been both clear and, for the believer, unsettling. A good example is the examination in Book One of the general philosophical principle 'that *whatever begins to exist, must have a cause of existence*' (*T* 78). That principle was an essential premise in the case for the necessary existence of a creator God, but, according to Hume, there was no demonstrative argument capable of proving it to be true. Hume also doubted the coherence of the idea of an immaterial soul, and argued that it had no more to recommend it than the materialism of the 'famous atheist' Spinoza (*T* 241).

The overall tendency of the *Treatise*, as we saw in Chapter 1, was to direct enquiry away from metaphysical matters, and towards empirical questions concerning ordinary life. Yet the reader who moved on from the *Treatise* to the essays that Hume wrote in the 1740s would have looked in vain for unequivocally positive treatment of what was, for most men and women in the 18th century, the most important dimension of human existence. Most of the references to religion in the essays are critical in tone. In a Calvinist country like Scotland, hostility to prevailing attitudes was implicit in Hume's remark in 'Of the Dignity or Meanness of Human Nature' that he was 'of the opinion, that the sentiments of those, who are inclined to think favourably of mankind, are more advantageous to virtue, than the contrary principles, which give us a mean opinion of our nature' (*EMPL* 81). In an essay 'Of Superstition and Enthusiasm', Hume identifies two species of false religion, one that sounds like Catholicism, one that sounds like Protestantism, and leaves unclear the nature of the true religion that is an instance of neither.

Superstitious fear of the unknown, Hume argues in that essay, generates a disposition to place faith in 'ceremonies, observances, mortifications, sacrifices, presents, or in any practice, however absurd or frivolous, which either folly or knavery recommends to a blind and terrified credulity' (*EMPL* 74). The enthusiast's confidence in being the direct recipient of divine favour, on the other hand, leads to a state of frenzy in which reason and morality are dispensed with in favour of the guidance supposedly provided by inspiration from above. These two corruptions of religion, Hume points out, have different and opposing political consequences. While superstition gives rise to the dominion of priests, the spirit of enthusiasm is the spirit of liberty, insofar as it valorizes the individual conscience and promotes the cause of toleration. In the essay 'Of Parties in General', however, Hume describes how, even in non-Catholic countries, religious differences are crucial to the process whereby the natural opposition of 'parties from interest' is turned into the much more complex, and much more dangerous, opposition of 'parties from principle'.

More hostile still was a footnote on the priestly vocation in the essay 'Of National Characters'. Hume claims there that few people—'or none'—have a propensity to religion sufficient in degree and constancy to support them in their calling. Priests, therefore, are always at war with their natural inclinations, and sustain the appearance of dedication and fervour only 'by a continued grimace and hypocrisy' (*EMPL* 200). Moreover, vices such as ambition, pride, rancour, and vindictiveness tend to be inflamed among clergymen, so that it is wise for any government to be always on guard against their machinations. This did not mean that it was impossible for ministers to be virtuous. What it meant was that the humane, humble, and moderate priest was beholden for those virtues 'to nature or reflection, not to the genius of his calling' (*EMPL* 201).

A reputation for irreligion was a part of what denied Hume the Edinburgh professorship of moral philosophy in 1744–5. The case against his candidacy was constructed out of passages from the *Treatise* which supposedly revealed 'universal Scepticism', 'Principles leading to downright Atheism', and 'Errors concerning the very Being and Existence of a God'. After his theory of the understanding had been very publicly traduced in this way, Hume perhaps felt that he had nothing to lose by being more open about what he took to be the consequences of his scepticism for religious belief. In *An Enquiry concerning Human Understanding* he included not only a section on miracles, but also a section denying the possibility of inferring intelligence and design from what we experience of the order of nature. The point, he claimed, was that the real foundation of religion was not reason but faith. Then, during the same period when he wrote *An Enquiry concerning the Principles of Morals* and *Political Discourses*, he composed the first draft of a much lengthier exploration of the possibility of giving a rational basis to belief in a creator God with traditional attributes such as wisdom and omnipotence. *Dialogues concerning Natural Religion*, however, would not be published until after Hume's death.

Miraculous Christianity

Hume devised the principal argument of 'Of Miracles' while he was in La Flèche writing the *Treatise*. It could be that he had been reading French attempts to establish the truths revealed in the Gospels using recent philosophical work on evidence and probability. He would almost certainly have read *Logic, or, the Art of Thinking* by Antoine Arnauld and Pierre Nicole, and taken note of how it treated the key episodes in early Christianity as historical events to which rules concerning the credibility of testimony could be applied in the same way as to events in secular history. What Arnauld and Nicole sought to show was that it is reasonable to accept the testimony of the Gospels despite the inherent implausibility of some of the stories they recounted. Hume describes in a letter how, during a conversation with a Jesuit priest, it occurred to him that this could not possibly be right

(*LDH* i 361). For he had developed a quite different conception of probability, according to which the evidence *against* the truth of a story of a miracle is always bound to be at least as strong as the evidence *for* its truth, regardless of the apparent reliability of testimony in question.

The issue here was not the abstract metaphysical question of whether or not miracles are *possible*. The general scepticism about metaphysics which Hume developed in the *Treatise* made it impossible for him to answer that question either way. The issue, rather, was reports of miracles, and whether experience can ever provide reason to believe them. The way to begin, then, was with a consideration of testimony in general. What makes it reasonable, in normal circumstances, to believe testimony is the fact, established by experience, that human beings are usually inclined to tell the truth, and that they are 'sensible to shame, when detected in a falsehood' (*E* 112). This is sufficient for there to be a presumption in favour of believing people, even complete strangers whose reliability we have no way of knowing. But it does not follow that it is reasonable to believe whatever one is told. For we do, of course, have experience of people lying, or being deceived. We have to balance experience of humankind's general veracity against the particularities of the situation, both with regard to the person giving the testimony and with regard to the story we are being told. In some cases, the result will be that we are unable to believe that story. Hume's argument was that belief in a story of a miracle will always be irrational, regardless of the apparent reliability of the person recounting the story.

It was precisely Hume's sceptical account of belief—his picture of our ignorance of the causal powers possessed by things in themselves, and of belief as the product of custom and habit—that enabled him to reach this conclusion. Belief about matters of fact, about what does and can happen in the world, is shaped entirely by experience. In other words, it is shaped by repeated instance of conjunctions of types of event. So where the matter of a fact reported in a piece of testimony is such as has rarely been observed, the degree of belief is bound to be minimal. And where there has been no experience at all, we have no idea what to believe. It is natural, for example, for someone who has never seen water freeze not to believe stories of water turning solid so that people can walk upon it. Now, a miracle is, by definition, not just an unusual event, or an event that cannot be explained because of an incomplete understanding of the laws of nature, but an event that is directly contrary to the laws of nature. A miracle is an interruption of the natural order of things, caused directly by God. 'There must, therefore,' Hume points out, 'be a uniform experience against every miraculous event, otherwise the event would not merit that appellation' (*E* 115). Our experience of the world speaks uniformly and unambiguously in favour of the falsity of any and every purported account of miraculous events.

It is worth emphasizing that this was not meant by Hume as a way of proving that miracles never happen. Instead, it was meant to show that reasonable people, when faced with a report of a miracle, will always find the report incredible. For all of their experience of the world will be against it—and (so Hume had shown in the *Treatise*) they have nothing *other* than experience on which to decide what to believe. It is possible, in principle, for uniform experience against every miraculous event to be countered by uniform experience in favour of the reliability of the particular person providing the testimony in question. Then the reasonable person will not know what to believe, and will suspend judgement altogether. But, Hume goes on to argue, in fact there is no case where it is just as likely that the report of the miracle is true as that it is false. In fact there are always reasons to doubt the veracity or sincerity of a reporter of a miracle, even when one puts the intrinsic incredibility of the report to one side.

No account of a miracle, according to Hume, is supported by a number of educated, honest, and disinterested witnesses sufficient to make it unreasonable to believe that the account is false. Then there is the fact that people like to tell stories that will elicit surprise and wonder in their audience, together with the fact that people like being surprised and made to wonder, and the fact that people who tell stories know that about their audiences. It is surely significant, furthermore, that reports of miracles are especially prevalent, as Hume put it, 'among ignorant and barbarous nations', and that where such reports prevail among civilized peoples, it will be found that they were transmitted by 'ignorant and barbarous ancestors' (*E* 119). And, finally, it stands to be noted that every report of a miracle taken as support of a particular religion is directly contradicted by all reports of miracles taken as support of other religions. At least, this is so on the assumption, which of course every monotheism makes, that only one religion can be true.

Hume's conclusion is that it is a mistake to imagine that the Gospels might provide historical evidence of the actuality of Christ's miracles, and hence of the truth of Christ's redemptive message. 'Our most holy religion', Hume declares, 'is founded on *Faith*, not reason' (*E* 130). Christian belief is itself a miracle, a subversion of reason such as could only be effected by God himself. It is not clear how seriously Hume imagined his reader would take this as a recommendation to restrain reason in order to make room for faith. He surely knew that 'Of Miracles' would be taken by most readers as suggesting that the whole of Christianity was a superstitious delusion on a par with stories of the curative capacities of the tomb of the abbé de Paris or of the Emperor Vespasian's spittle.

Experimental theism

It was not unusual in the early 18th century to combine scepticism about the literal truth of the Bible with confidence in the possibility of a religion of reason that was 'natural' in the sense that it was available to all human beings, regardless of whether or not they had heard of Jesus Christ. Where in the past natural religion

had been taken to be the product of a priori reasoning—based, for
example, on the maxim that every beginning of existence had to
have a cause—the success of 'experimental philosophy' in the
age of Harvey, Boyle, and Newton had encouraged some to
think that science by itself provided conclusive reasons to believe
in an intelligent creator of the universe. In 1748 the Scottish
mathematician Colin Maclaurin claimed that 'The plain argument
for the existence of the Deity, obvious to all and carrying
irresistible conviction with it, is from the evident contrivance and
fitness of things for one another which we meet with throughout
all the parts of the universe.' This was an argument from the
apparent adjustment of means to ends revealed everywhere in
nature. The universe looked like a work of human manufacture,
only on an infinitely larger scale, and it therefore seemed plausible
to suppose that its creator had an intelligence analogous to,
though again infinitely greater than, the intelligence of the
human mind.

The question was whether this propensity to believe was, as Hume
put it in a letter, 'somewhat different from our Inclination to find
our own Figures in the Clouds, our Face in the Moon, our Passions
& Sentiments even in inanimate matter' (*LDH* i 155). The
argument to design had yet to be given a formal statement. In the
manuscript that was eventually published as *Dialogues concerning
Natural Religion*, Hume stages a discussion of the argument
between three characters, one of whom tries to state it as clearly
and convincingly as possible, while the other two subject it to
probing criticism. The defender of the argument, Cleanthes, is
described as possessing an 'accurate philosophical turn' (*DNH*
30). One of the critics, Demea, attacks the argument from the
point of view of 'rigid inflexible orthodoxy'—which means, from
the point of view of the Calvinism that had been prevalent in
Scotland since the Reformation. Such Calvinism preferred the
certainties of a priori argument to the probabilism of experimental
religion, but rested confidence ultimately in man's 'consciousness
of his imbecility and misery' (*DNH* 95). Philo, the other critic, is

said to be 'careless' in his scepticism. In other words, he has no particular cause to defend, and is interested only in where the argument leads. Most readers suppose that Philo speaks for Hume himself. As we will see, such an assumption is not completely unproblematic.

All three participants agree at the outset that the question under discussion is not the existence but the nature of God. That is, they accept that the universe has a cause responsible for its creation and its preservation through time. They differ with respect to what can be known about that cause, and how. Cleanthes' position is that experience—ordinary everyday experience combined with the results of scientific investigation—plainly tells us that the world is, in his own words, 'nothing but one great machine, subdivided into an infinite number of lesser machines, which again admit of subdivisions, to a degree beyond what human senses and faculties can trace and explain' (*DNH* 45). Our legs, for example, are perfectly contrived for walking and climbing. Every part of the eye is designed to make sight possible. In both their physiology and their passions, 'and the whole course of life before and after generation', the male and female of each species appear intended together for that species' propagation. Everywhere we look, we see order, proportion, and the arrangement of parts to serve the purposes of a larger whole. The similarity between the works of nature and works of human art is, Cleanthes insists, self-evident and undeniable. 'What more is requisite', he asks, 'to show an analogy between their causes, and to ascertain the origin of all things from a divine purpose and intention?' (*DNH* 54).

Demea objects that this argument gives up on 'the adorable mysteriousness of the divine nature' (*DNH* 47). According to him, it is of the essence of religion that God should be both certain in his existence and unknowable in his wisdom and justice. Philo, too, objects to what he terms Cleanthes' 'anthropomorphitism'. A more careful assessment of what we know about the universe shows that the analogy between nature and works of human contrivance is much, much weaker than Cleanthes claims. Cleanthes wants to make *experience* the basis of our knowledge of the attributes of God. And, unfortunately for the purposes of theological argument, our experience is too limited for any sure conjecture about the cause of the universe. We know only one part of that universe. In other parts there may be principles of operation quite different from human intelligence, and it may be that it is by one or other of those unknown principles that God's nature is to be known. No matter how well we know our part of the universe, we only know it now, and have no idea either of what it might have been like in its 'embryo-state' or of what it might be developing into. Any safe causal hypothesis in experimental science depends on an amount of observation of the pairings of like causes with like effects, but, plainly enough, no one has ever observed the generation of a universe.

Philo goes on to argue that none of the traditional attributes of God can be established by experimental means. Everything that we encounter in the world is finite, and so Cleanthes' style of reasoning must renounce any claim to be able to show God's infinity. There are many ways in which the world appears not to be perfect. Even if we allow that this is a merely superficial perspective on things and that what appear to be faults (bodily pains, for example) are in reality aspects of perfection, still, there may well be faults that we know nothing about, and that cannot be explained away in this fashion. Even if the world were completely perfect, could we be sure that its perfections were due to perfection on the part of its maker? 'Many worlds might have been botched and bungled, throughout an eternity, ere this system was struck out: Much labour lost: Many fruitless trials made: And a slow, but continued improvement carried on during infinite ages in the art of world-making' (*DNH* 69). Nor is there any firmer evidence of the unity of God. A house is made by many men. Why should the universe not be the work of many deities? Or if that seems extravagant, perhaps two deities, one male and one female?

This last question leads to others in a similar vein. Cleanthes claims that the universe is like a machine. But perhaps that is a false analogy. Perhaps the universe is better compared to a living creature, an animal, or a vegetable. It might well be said to be like an organized body, with an inherent principle of life and motion, a continual but regular circulation of matter and repair of damage, each part working incessantly to preserve itself and thereby preserving the whole. And its manner of generation might therefore be supposed to be more like that of a living organism than that of a house or a loom. As the dialogue goes on, Philo produces a series of increasingly bizarre variations on this theme, intended to show that there is a range of possible explanations for the universe each just as empirically plausible as the hypothesis with which Cleanthes began. The only conclusion to reach, Philo says, is that 'we have no *data* to establish any system of cosmogony. Our experience, so imperfect in itself, and so limited in both extent and duration, can afford us no probable conjecture concerning the whole of things' (*DNH* 79). The rational course of action, when it comes to the nature of the cause of the universe, is a total suspense of judgement. Philo amplifies this triumph of scepticism by proceeding to a demolition of the traditional kind of a priori proof of God's existence favoured by Demea, followed by an assault on all attempts to explain away the existence of evil, whether natural or moral.

It puzzles many readers of the *Dialogues* that in the work's final part, Philo appears to step back from a position of pure scepticism. No one, he tells Cleanthes, has a deeper sense of religion than he does. 'A purpose, an intention, a design', he says, 'strikes everywhere the most careless, the most stupid thinker; and no man can be so hardened in absurd systems, as at all times to reject it' (*DNH* 116). It seems that here, as at the end of Book One of the *Treatise*, a total suspense of judgement is impossible. Making a special effort, one can be a sceptic some of the time, perhaps, but the rest of the time a natural tendency to belief reasserts itself. Does this mean that Hume holds that scepticism about natural religion is as artificial and ultimately untenable as, say, scepticism about the existence of an external world? Or is he merely dissimulating here, pretending for prudential reasons to endorse a commonsensical position that, in fact, he has completely undermined in the main part of the text?

These are not the only possible conclusions to draw. It could be that all that Philo is admitting is that the works of nature *look* as though they are the work of an intelligent designer. It is possible, with some ingenuity, to come up with explanatory hypotheses that have an equal amount of empirical evidence, but the first and most natural thing to think about the world around us is that all of it was contrived by a being with ideas and purposes analogous to those of human beings in their far simpler and inferior works of art and manufacture. The theist will accept, in fact insist, that, even so, there is an immeasurable difference between the human and the divine mind. For his part, the sceptic will not deny, given the 'coherence and apparent sympathy' in all the parts of nature, that there is likely to be some essential similarity between the different fundamental principles at work in those different parts. And if the sceptic admits that, as he must, then he will not deny that it is 'probable, that the principle, which first arranged, and still maintains order in this universe, bears...also some remote inconceivable analogy to the other operations of nature, and among the rest to the œconomy of human mind and thought' (*DNH* 120). All the theist and sceptic are disagreeing about is exactly how immeasurably different the cause of the universe is from the human mind.

What Philo is trying to do here, perhaps, is to spell out the difference between *scepticism* on the one hand, and *atheism* on the other. He wants to make it clear that unlike the atheist, he is not offering a substantive thesis intended as an explanation of the appearance of contrivance in the world as we experience it. His position is *compatible* with theism, but it is not in itself a species of theism in any usual sense of the word. Philo emphasizes this

8. From the manuscript of *Dialogues concerning Natural Religion*.

when, in the last pages of the *Dialogues*, he denies that his extremely minimal 'true religion' has any implications whatsoever for how life ought to be lived. Cleanthes says that '[r]eligion, however corrupted, is still better than no religion at all' (*DNH* 121). He thinks that the idea of a life after death, in particular, is a necessary support of morality, because people's commitment to moral principles can only be guaranteed if they believe that there will be punishment and reward in the life that follows this one. Philo—and, certainly, Hume himself—could not disagree more. There is no need to pretend that the content of true religion is any more substantial than it really is. Most people do not need positive religious commitment of any kind to maintain their attachment to what, in the *Enquiry concerning the Principles of Morals*, Hume called 'the *party* of human-kind against vice or disorder, its common enemy' (*E* 275). Religion which claims to have more content than true religion can have is, in reality, almost always *worse* than no religion at all.

The origin of religion in human nature

If, as Hume argues in both 'Of Miracles' and *Dialogues concerning Natural Religion* (Figure 8), religion had no foundation in reason, then why has religious belief been a feature of almost every society in human history? This is the question that Hume addresses in 'The Natural History of Religion'. It is not clear when he wrote this work, but it may have been yet another product of the time he spent at home in Chirnside between 1749 and 1751. It was published in 1757, part of a collection entitled *Four Dissertations* that also included Hume's rewrite of Book Two of the *Treatise*. This is unlikely to have been a coincidence, since the origin of religion in the passions was a major theme of the 'Natural History'. Another major theme was the morally pernicious consequences of superstition.

A *natural* history of religion considered religion as a merely natural phenomenon, rather than as a set of doctrines and practices derived directly from divine revelation. It considered religion as an element of the process whereby human society improved, as Hume put it, 'from rude beginnings to a state of greater perfection' (*DNH* 135). It portrayed religion as the product, like other aspects of culture, of the interaction between the principles of human nature and the physical environment in which early human beings found themselves placed. The fact that, 'if travellers and historians may be credited', some nations have no sentiments of religion, and that there are so many different forms of religion, suggested to Hume that religion does *not* begin in 'an original or primary impression of nature, such as gives rise to self-love, affection between the sexes, love of progeny, gratitude, resentment'. It is, rather, an effect of one or more of those primary principles, and as such 'may easily be perverted by various accidents and causes' (*DNH* 134).

It was usual, both among apologists for Christianity and among proponents of a 'natural' religion of reason, to suppose that the earliest religion had been monotheistic. Pagan polytheism, on this view, was a corruption of religion in its original and pure form. Hume turns this narrative on its head. He argues that the evidence provided by history and by the practices of 'the savage tribes of America, Africa, and Asia' (*DNH* 135) suggests that polytheism and idolatry were the first manifestations of the religious impulse. They were probably an expression of ignorance and an acute sense of precariousness on the part of the earliest human communities. The first ideas of religion arose from fear, and from hope that something could be done to assuage that fear. In the most primitive societies, it must have seemed almost entirely out of human control whether there was life or death, health or sickness, plenty or want. People therefore looked to supernatural powers to explain the vicissitudes of existence, and looked to them also for means of making life easier to endure. Inevitably, they supposed that those powers were, though superior in understanding and power, much like them in their motivations and satisfactions.

Monotheism replaced polytheism not as a result of a new appreciation of the arguments of natural religion, but rather as a further expression of the tendency to project human characteristics onto supernatural powers. In idolatrous nations it would have happened that one god was selected as the object of special worship and adoration. This god was imagined to be particularly concerned with the good of one particular people. Alternatively, he was imagined to be more powerful than the other gods, and to rule over them like a king over inferior magistrates. Seeking to please this one god with praise and flattery, his votaries dreamed up ever more impressive titles for him, until they got to the point where their language was full of his infinity, unity, and simplicity. At the same time, however, they continued to believe that he had passions like a human being, and needed to be pleased and placated, by any number of absurd rites and rituals. Not seeing the contradiction here, people allowed themselves to believe, for example, that the best way to win God's favour for your children was 'to cut off from them, while infants, a little bit of skin, about half the breadth of a farthing', or that the wearing of the scapular was the secret to recommending yourself to an infinite being who existed from eternity to eternity (*DNH* 158).

To see religion in the context of human passions was to see it as something unstable and always changing. It was natural, Hume argued, that people's needs could not long be answered by the idea of a God whose infinitude and perfection served ultimately to remove him from their comprehension. The most fundamental need of all is the need for happiness, and, in order to think of religion as a means of achieving happiness, mediators and subordinate agents were invented to interpose between man and God. These in turn became themselves the object of reverence and worship, and thus, with such things as the cult of the Virgin and altars dedicated to saints, monotheism effectively turned back into polytheism. 'It is remarkable', Hume observed, 'that the principles of religion have a kind of flux and reflux in the human mind, and that men have a tendency to rise from idolatry to theism, and to sink again from theism into idolatry' (*DNH* 158). Although Hume did not make the point himself, it was obvious that the Protestant Reformation could, from this point of view, be seen as just another episode in the endless cycle, a reassertion of monotheism that would, in turn, be followed by a return to polytheism.

Polytheism is always absurd, but at least it is generally tolerant of diversity in religious belief and practice. It sits lightly on the mind, and is seldom the cause of fanaticism or violence. Monotheism, by contrast, is according to Hume inherently intolerant. History is full of the bloody consequences of cleaving to a single, jealous God. Those consequences are more shocking than even the human sacrifices that used to be required by some pagan religions. Whereas sacrificial victims were selected at random, it was specifically virtue, knowledge, and the love of liberty that most offended the Roman Catholic inquisition, so much so that countries visited by the inquisitors were left 'in the most shameful ignorance, corruption, and bondage' (*DNH* 163). Things were different in Protestant countries, and the Dutch Republic and England in particular were remarkable for their tolerance of dissent. But, Hume insists, such tolerance was the result of the efforts of politicians, always working in opposition to the narrow, sectarian sentiments of priests.

Polytheism, moreover, with its limited and fallible divinities, encourages human beings to think they can emulate their gods—'[h]ence activity, spirit, courage, magnanimity, love of liberty, and all the virtues which aggrandize a people' (*DNH* 163–4). The virtues inspired by monotheism are very different. Instead of fights with monsters, resistance to tyrants, and all-out defence of the *patria*, there are the 'monkish virtues' that Hume excoriated in the *Enquiry concerning the Principles of Morals*. The morality of monotheism is a morality of 'whippings and fastings, cowardice and humility, abject submission and slavish obedience' (*DNH* 164). It saps the spirit and debases the character. Its inevitable corruption of the sentiments is intensified by the suspicion that what God most wants from his votaries is not what is natural and instinctive, but instead what goes most violently against the grain of human inclination. This explains the common observation that fervour and strictness of religion are very far from being a reliable sign of a person's good moral character. It also explains the fact that, far from making people happy, religion engenders anxiety, fear, and self-loathing.

Hume chose to publish 'The Natural History of Religion' at a moment when his friends among the 'moderate' wing of the Church of Scotland were under intense pressure from traditionalist members of the religious establishment. What had particularly provoked the anger of the 'orthodox' was the success of a play—a blank verse tragedy called *Douglas*—not only written by a minister, but enthusiastically attended, even on Sundays, by a large proportion of the clergy of Edinburgh and its surrounding towns and villages. At the same time moves were made to expel Hume from the Church, in order, presumably, to provoke his friends into defending him. (They did defend him, and the moves failed.) Hume's response was to publish *Four Dissertations* with a fulsome dedication to John Home, the author of the offending play. He also added to the *Natural History* a long footnote mocking the idea that a theatre might be 'the porch of hell', and using the doctrine of predestination, still fervently preached by traditionalists in Scotland, as a prime example of the immorality of modern religion. It increased the piquancy of this attack on orthodoxy that the footnote was almost entirely taken up with a quotation from a Scottish writer, Andrew Ramsay, who himself, in Hume's ambiguous words, 'had so laudable an inclination to be orthodox, that his reason never found any difficulty, even in the doctrines which free thinkers scruple the most, the trinity, incarnation, and satisfaction' (*DNH* 191). What made Ramsay object to predestination was, simply, his 'humanity'.

The future of religion

Once he had completed *The History of England*, Hume found himself unsure what to do next. He considered publishing *Dialogues concerning Natural Religion*, but was talked out of it by friends, probably because they did not want more trouble from the traditionalists in the Church of Scotland. Another possibility was to add to the *History* by bringing the narrative forward into the 18th century, perhaps to the accession of George I. The renewal of factional politics in England, though, made that an unappealing prospect. It would have required access to private papers held in the archives of the nobility, and Hume was not sure that such access would be granted him. When the offer came, then, of a job as secretary to the British ambassador to France, Hume happily accepted. He was in Paris from 1763 until 1766. There he got to know many of the great men and women of the French Enlightenment, but found most of them, intellectually speaking, not to his taste. They were zealous, even violent, in their opinions, where Hume was detached and disengaged. Edward Gibbon recounted how d'Holbach, La Mettrie, and their friends 'laughed at the scepticism of Hume, preached the tenets of atheism with the bigotry of dogmatists, and damned all believers with ridicule and contempt'.

For the French *philosophes*, religion remained a powerful enemy of the progress of reason and liberty. The *Encyclopédie*, the great vehicle of Enlightenment engineered by Diderot and d'Alembert, had been suppressed in 1759 and placed on the Church's Index of forbidden books. Both Rousseau's *Émile* and *The Social Contract* were condemned by the Parliament of Paris in 1762. Many of what we now think of as the major works of 18th-century French thought had to be published clandestinely outside France, or could not be published at all. The situation in Britain was, from Hume's point of view, very different. For centuries, in the ages of superstition, Britain too had been subject to the overweening efforts of popes and bishops to influence its political affairs. Then in the 17th century it had seen a great explosion of enthusiasm. In the *History of England* Hume gave detailed accounts of the violent and cruel consequences of both forms of religious excess. He also described how, in a magnificent example of an unintended and unforeseen consequence, the often bizarre and always extreme appetite for religious change on the part of the Puritan element of the House of the Commons in the 1630s and 1640s contained the seeds of the Revolution of 1688. But as this process worked itself through, England's religious fervour had burnt itself out to almost nothing. In 1752 Hume added to his essay 'Of National Characters' a passage in which he claimed that the British were 'now settled into the most cool indifference with regard to religious matters, that is to be found in any nation in the world' (*EMPL* 206).

Evidence for the truth of this claim was provided by the 'Wilkes and Liberty' riots in London in the late 1760s. While Hume hated everything to do with Wilkes and his mob of supporters, it had to be admitted that religion—apart from routine anti-Catholicism—was completely absent from these upheavals. Neither Wilkes nor his supporters claimed, in the manner of Cromwell and his followers in the New Model Army, to be inspired by divine assurance of the justice of their cause. Wilkes, in fact, had the reputation of being a libertine, possibly even an atheist.

In an essay from 1741 about the future of the British form of government, Hume detected a sudden change in public opinion caused by the progress of learning and liberty. 'Most people, in this island', he claimed, 'have divested themselves of all superstitious reverence to names and authority: The clergy have much lost their credit: Their pretensions and doctrines have been ridiculed; and even religion can scarce support itself in the world' (*EMPL* 51). It was not, of course, that the British had suddenly all become unbelievers. But they were not any longer prepared to fight over religious matters, and were prepared to tolerate a relatively large amount of diversity in doctrine and practice. Voltaire might have had an explanation of this development in his picture of Christians, Jews, and Muslims at the London Stock Exchange, all devoted to the religion of making money, and reserving the name of infidel only for bankrupts.

In Scotland, less commercially developed as it was than England, the spirit of religion was, for the moment at least, stronger. Hence the trouble made for Hume and the Church of Scotland's moderates in the 1750s, and hence, perhaps, Hume's continuing unwillingness to publish the *Dialogues*. Yet the days were long gone when the Church could inflict civil penalties on those judged to be insufficient in their adherence to the Westminster Confession of Faith. The most that the orthodox could have visited upon Hume was the social awkwardness of not being able to be received in the houses of his friends in Edinburgh. To Hume, the efforts of his enemies never seemed anything more than absurd. The more the devout attempted to interfere in moral and political affairs, the more ridiculous they made themselves appear. There was nothing like the Calas Affair to persuade him to follow Voltaire in coming to see religious bigotry as a genuine threat to the modern age's success in the improvement of manners and morals.

Adam Smith reported in a letter that on his deathbed Hume joked about asking Charon to delay taking him across the Styx to the underworld until he had 'the pleasure of seeing the churches shut up, and the Clergy sent about their business'. When the letter was later published together with Hume's brief autobiography, the joke was toned down, with Hume made to say that what he desired was to witness 'the downfall of some of the prevailing systems of superstition'. In both texts, though, Hume acknowledges that Charon's reply would be that he would have to wait hundreds of years for anything to change. In all probability Hume found it difficult so much as to imagine what a world without organized religion would look like. When, in one of the essays in *Political Discourses*, he sketched his own 'idea of a perfect commonwealth', he included a church organized along Presbyterian lines, with an autonomous ecclesiastical court for each county—though with the provision that the civil magistrate could take any case away from the church courts, and could try or suspend any of the presbyters who manned them (see *EMPL* 520).

The implication of the 'Natural History of Religion' was that religion is so deeply intertwined with some of the most basic human passions that, even though it does not spring from a primary principle of human nature, it can be expected to manifest itself, in some form or other, in any conceivable future of the human race. It seems unlikely that Hume imagined that the sceptical arguments of 'Of Miracles' and the *Dialogues* would have much of an effect on the general propensity of human beings to invent systems of superstition to calm their anxieties and give plausibility to their hopes. On his account of human nature, after all, reason is nothing more than 'the slave of the passions'—'and

can never pretend to any other office than to serve and obey them'
(*T* 415). The most that could realistically be expected was that,
with the development of political stability and the growth of
material prosperity, religious sentiments would continue to
diminish in intensity, and so have ever fewer harmful moral and
political effects.

Postscript

The History of England, published in complete form in 1762, was in one sense the end of Hume's career as an author. He wrote only a handful of miscellaneous pieces in the years that followed. The longest of them was a self-justifying account (in French) of the dramatic deterioration of the friendship he had formed with Jean-Jacques Rousseau at the end of his time in Paris, written in order to pre-empt Rousseau's publication of his side of the story. For reasons that are not at all clear, Hume regarded this quarrel as 'the most critical affair, which, during the whole course of my life, I have been engaged in' (*LDH* ii 54). In its aftermath he returned to public service, this time as an Under-Secretary of State in the Northern Department, responsible for government business in northern Europe. But after two years in London he headed back to Edinburgh, and had a grand house built in the city's recently developed New Town. He was now, thanks to a combination of the success of the *History* and the pensions attached to the various military and government positions he had held, a very wealthy man. But in the spring of 1775 he fell seriously ill with a bowel disease that, after a painful decline which he bore with remarkable equanimity, killed him in August 1776.

In another sense, the publication of *The History of England* was very far from the end of Hume's literary career. Hume was a compulsive rereader of his own books, and took the opportunity

9. Hume's tomb on Calton Hill by Aeneas Macpherson, 1789.

presented by each new edition to make alterations both major and very minor. He joked to his publisher William Strahan that 'one half of a man's life is too little to write a book, and the other half too little to correct it' (*LDH* ii 234, 304). So far as he himself was concerned, Hume's achievement as an author was contained in just two works, the *History*, and a collection of what he described as his 'philosophical' writings, entitled *Essays and Treatises on Several Subjects*. (The choice of title was strange, given that the *Essays and Treatises* contained almost everything Hume wrote *apart* from *A Treatise of Human Nature*.) He wanted these two works to be as correct as he could possibly make them. His final letter to Strahan, written two weeks before his death, was a request for a small change to be made to the *Enquiry concerning the Principles of Morals*.

The very last thing that Hume wrote was a brief autobiography, to be prefixed to future editions of his works. 'My Own Life' is a complex and enigmatic text. Part of its point, in a final dig at the 'orthodox', was to show that it was possible for the religious sceptic to die a calm and even happy death. Another thing that Hume wanted to make clear was that the challenges he had issued to received opinion in philosophy, morals, politics, history, and religion had not prevented him from making a great deal of money from his books. 'My Own Life' gave a very selective account of Hume's career, but contained a fairly detailed description of his progress from 'a very rigid frugality' to the 'opulence' and 'superfluity' of 'a Revenue of a 1000 pounds a year'. Just as striking, however, is the pose that Hume strikes of having been constantly embattled, always misunderstood, and permanently on the receiving end of disapprobation—'and even Detestation'. This is a picture of Hume's place in 18th-century letters that too many of his readers have been willing to accept. It is, at best, only half the truth.

Twice in 'My Own Life' Hume mentions the rough treatment he had received at the hands of the circle of Bishop William Warburton. He singles out for special complaint Richard Hurd's *Remarks on Mr Hume's Natural History of Religion*, as being full of 'the illiberal Petulance, Arrogance, and Scurrility, which distinguishes the Warburtonian School'. He could have objected also to the misrepresentations and *ad hominem* attacks contained in the Aberdonian philosopher James Beattie's *Essay on the Nature and Immutability of Truth*, a book whose success earned its author an honorary degree from Oxford and a pension from the king. He was well aware of the dislike he had excited in Samuel Johnson, who told James Boswell that Hume was a man entirely consumed by vanity, and that Hume's report of his state of mind on his deathbed was the work either of a liar or of a madman. The problem with 'My Own Life' is that it pretends that this kind of thing was all there was to the reception of Hume's writings in his lifetime. The only positive responses it mentions are those of the primates of England and Ireland to the first volume of the *History*—'which', as Hume puts it, 'seem two odd Exceptions'.

What goes unmentioned in Hume's autobiography is the almost universal acclaim that he won among the leading intellectuals of his day. Both philosophers and historians, in Scotland, England, France, and further afield in Europe and in America, engaged seriously with his work. The *Treatise*, as Hume does not fail to mention in 'My Own Life', was not a great success. But more or less everything that Hume wrote afterwards was read by more or less everyone, and the reactions of Warburton, Hurd, Beattie, and Johnson were not representative. In Scotland, Hume's works were replied to in detail by George Campbell, Lord Kames, Thomas Reid, Adam Smith, and Robert Wallace. Richard Price in England wrote a careful response to 'Of Miracles', and Hume and Josiah Tucker debated the comparative trading advantages of poor countries over rich ones. Hume was an inspiration to both Edmund Burke and Edward Gibbon. He was an extraordinary success among the French *philosophes*. He became friends with Benjamin Franklin, and was read by those on both sides of the American Revolution. In 1767 a friend told him that he 'never met with any person who could pretend to any degree of taste & sense who did not look upon your work to be as entertaining and instructive as that of almost any other author which the world has ever produced'.

Hume, in other words, was at the very centre of the Enlightenment. This does not mean that his works expressed the views of the Enlightenment's intellectual mainstream. They did not. For the most part—Adam Smith in *The Wealth of Nations* was a rare exception—his contemporaries responded to him in order to disagree. But from Hume's point of view, that was exactly as it should be. He did not write in order to gain disciples or create a school. What he wanted, instead, was open debate about all issues of importance to modern men and women, debate conducted according to the highest intellectual standards, but also with civility, generosity, and good humour. It may be that the attempt of Hume and his contemporaries to create a discursive space in which such debate was possible gives us the best definition of what the Enlightenment was. It may also be the best answer to the question of why the Enlightenment still matters.

References

Chapter 1: Human nature

'they that examine into the Nature of Man': Bernard Mandeville,
    The Fable of the Bees, ed. F. B. Kaye, 2 vols (Oxford University
    Press, 1924), vol. i, pp. 3–4.
'One of the greatest reasons why so few People understand
    themselves': Mandeville, *Fable*, ed. Kaye, vol. i, p. 39.
'Hobbes had described pride': Thomas Hobbes, *Leviathan*, ed.
    Richard Tuck, revised student edition (Cambridge University
    Press, 1996), p. 88.
'as Samuel Johnson put it': Samuel Johnson, *A Dictionary of the
    English Language* (London, 1755), 'Moral'.
'a brief "abstract", or summary': Hume, *An Abstract of a Book Lately
    Published; Entituled, A Treatise of Human Nature* (London, 1740).
'susceptible of as accurate a disquisition, as the laws of motion':
    'Dissertation of the Passions', in Hume, *Four Dissertations*
    (Edinburgh, 1757), p. 181.

Chapter 2: Morality

'Hutcheson's inaugural lecture': Francis Hutcheson, 'On the Natural
    Sociability of Man', in *Logic, Metaphysics, and the Natural
    Sociability of Mankind*, trans. and ed. James Moore and Michael
    Silverthorne (Liberty Fund, 2006), pp. 93–4.
'brought philosophy out of the closets and libraries': *The Spectator*, ed.
    Donald F. Bond, 4 vols (Oxford University Press, 1965), vol. i, p. 44.
'compose half the world': *Spectator*, ed. Bond, vol. i, p. 21.

'the virtue of a woman', 'no self-denial': Adam Smith, *The Theory of Moral Sentiments*, ed. D. D. Raphael and Alan Macfie (Oxford University Press, 1976), pp. 190–91.

'More than once Hume declared that the *Enquiry* was his favourite': Hume, *Letters*, ed. Greig, vol. i, p. 227; 'My Own Life', ed. Gordon Brown, pp. 95–6.

'an early manuscript fragment': M. A. Stewart, 'An Early Fragment on Evil', in M. A. Stewart and J. P. Wright (eds), *Hume and Hume's Connexions* (Pennsylvania University Press, 1995), pp. 160–70.

'Turgot gave a lecture': 'A Philosophical Review of the Successive Stages of the Human Mind', in *Turgot on Progress, Sociology and Economics*, trans. and ed. Ronald L. Meek (Cambridge University Press, 1973).

Chapter 3: Politics

'Hume, Smith would remark, was the first writer': Adam Smith, *The Wealth of Nations*, ed. R. H. Campbell, A. S. Skinner, and W. B. Todd (Oxford University Press, 1976), p. 412.

'the only book of mine that was successful on the first publication': Hume, *My Own Life*, ed. Gordon Brown, p. 95.

'It was nonsense to claim, as Montesquieu did': Baron de Montesquieu, *The Spirit of the Laws*, trans. and ed. Anne Cohler, Basia Miller, and Harold Oldmixon (Cambridge University Press, 1989), pp. 165–6.

'Voltaire had noted': Voltaire, *Letters concerning the English Nation*, ed. Nicholas Cronk (Oxford World's Classics, 2009), pp. 110–11.

'Montesquieu had come to the same conclusion': *Spirit of the Laws*, trans. and ed. Cohler et al., p. 333.

Chapter 4: Religion

'The case against his candidacy': as summarized in Hume, *A Letter from a Gentleman to his Friend in Edinburgh* (Edinburgh, 1745).

'In 1748 Colin Maclaurin claimed': Colin Maclaurin, *An Account of Sir Isaac Newton's Discoveries* (London, 1748), p. 381.

'Edward Gibbon recounted how d'Holbach': Edward Gibbon, *Memoirs of my Life*, ed. Betty Radice (Penguin, 1984), p. 136.

'Voltaire might have had an explanation': Voltaire, *Letters concerning the English Nation*, ed. Cronk, p. 30.

'Adam Smith reported in a letter': *The Correspondence of Adam Smith*, ed. Ernest Campbell Mossner and Ian Simpson Ross (Oxford University Press, 1977), p. 163.

'the joke was toned down': the 'Letter from Adam Smith, LL.D. to William Strahan, Esq.' is often printed with 'My Own Life', e.g. *EMPL* xliii–xlix, *HE* i xxxv–xl.

Postscript

'a self-justifying account': *Exposé Succinct de la Contestation qui s'est Élevée entre M. Hume et M. Rousseau, Avec les Piéces Justificatives* (London, 1766).

'My Own Life': reprinted in many editions of Hume's works, e.g. *DNH* 3–10, *EMPL* xxxi–xli, *HE* i xvii–xxxiv, *LDH* i 1–7; but see esp. Hume, *My Own Life*, ed. Gordon Brown (2nd edn, Royal Society of Edinburgh, 2017), pp. 77–92 (a facsimile of the manuscript) and 93–9 (a transcription of the manuscript).

'who told James Boswell': James Boswell, *The Life of Samuel Johnson*, ed. David Womersley (Penguin, 2008), pp. 234, 314–15.

'In 1767 a friend told him': see James A. Harris, *Hume: An Intellectual Biography* (Cambridge University Press, 2015), pp. 472, 574 n. 62.

Further reading

Hume's works

Reliable texts of all of Hume's published works, including *The History of England*, are freely available on the Hume Texts Online website at <www.davidhume.org>. The best edition of *A Treatise of Human Nature* remains the one produced by L. A. Selby-Bigge in 1888, as revised by Peter Nidditch and published by Oxford University Press in 1978. It is still in print, as is Selby-Bigge's combined edition (again revised by Nidditch) of *An Enquiry concerning Human Understanding* and *An Enquiry concerning the Principles of Morals* (Oxford University Press, 1975). There have been several more recent editions of *An Enquiry concerning Human Understanding*, including one in the Oxford World's Classics series by Peter Millican (2008). There are also several recent editions of *Dialogues concerning Natural Religion*, including one in the Oxford World's Classics Series by J. C. A. Gaskin (1993), which also contains *The Natural History of Religion*. For the moment the most convenient edition of Hume's *Essays Moral, Political, and Literary* is published by Liberty Fund (edited by Eugene F. Miller, 1987). Liberty Fund is the publisher also of the only complete version of *The History of England* since the 19th century, printed in six volumes (foreword by William B. Todd, 1983). Oxford University Press is currently producing a new scholarly edition of all of Hume's works, including *The History of England*. For details of the volumes published so far, visit the 'Clarendon Hume Series' pages of the Oxford University Press website (<www.oup.com>). There is as yet no modern edition of Hume's correspondence, but Oxford University Press has kept in print both J. Y. T. Greig's 1932 *The Letters of David Hume* and Raymond Klibansky and Ernest C. Mossner's 1954 *New Letters of David Hume*.

Hume's life

Easily the best edition of 'My Own Life', complete with photographs of Hume's manuscript and full commentary, is by Iain Gordon Brown (second revised and expanded edition, Royal Society of Edinburgh, 2017). John Robertson's article on Hume in the *Oxford Dictionary of National Biography* is a reliable, concise account of Hume's life. The standard full biography is still Ernest Campbell Mossner, *The Life of David Hume*, revised edition (Oxford University Press, 1980). Mossner's focus is the man, not his ideas. The only intellectual biography is James A. Harris, *Hume: An Intellectual Biography* (Cambridge University Press, 2015).

Human nature

New life was breathed into the study of Hume's theory of human nature by Annette C. Baier, *A Progress of Sentiments: Reflections on Hume's* Treatise (Harvard University Press, 1991). The fullest account of Mandeville's impact on Hume is Mikko Tolonen, *Mandeville and Hume: Anatomists of Civil Society* (Voltaire Foundation, 2013). On Hume on the understanding, see David Owen, *Hume's Reason* (Oxford University Press, 1999), and Donald C. Ainslie, *Hume's True Scepticism* (Oxford University Press, 2015). On Hume on the passions, see Jane L. McIntyre, 'Hume's "New and Extraordinary" Account of the Passions', in Saul Traiger (ed.), *The Blackwell Guide to Hume's* Treatise (Blackwell Publishing, 2006), pp. 199–215, and Jacqueline A. Taylor, *Reflecting Subjects: Passion, Sympathy, and Society in Hume's Philosophy* (Oxford University Press, 2015). Context for Hume's claims about a single human nature and about Africans in relation to Europeans is provided by Aaron Garrett, 'Human Nature', in Knud Haakonssen (ed.), *The Cambridge History of Eighteenth-Century Philosophy* (Cambridge University Press, 2006), pp. 160–233, and Silvia Sebastiani, *The Scottish Enlightenment: Race, Gender and the Limits of Progress*, trans. Jeremy Carden (Palgrave Macmillan, 2013). For a fuller account of the *Treatise* along the lines sketched in Chapter 1, see James A. Harris, 'A Compleat Chain of Reasoning: Hume's Project in *A Treatise of Human Nature*, Books One and Two', *Proceedings of the Aristotelian Society* 109 (2009): 129–48.

Morality

A convincing exploration of the moral philosophy of Book 3 of
A Treatise of Human Nature is Rachel Cohon, *Hume's Morality:
Feeling and Fabrication* (Oxford University Press, 2008). Hume's
intentions as an essayist are well described in Nicholas Phillipson,
'Hume as Moralist: A Social Historian's Perspective', in S. C. Brown
(ed.), *Philosophers of the Enlightenment* (Harvester Press, 1979),
pp. 140–61; and in Mark Box, *The Suasive Art of David Hume*
(Princeton University Press, 1990). The practical dimension of Hume's
writings on morality is the focus also of Donald T. Siebert, *The Moral
Animus of David Hume* (University of Delaware Press, 1990). The best
account of the 18th-century background for Hume's moral thought is
Colin Heydt, *Moral Philosophy in Eighteenth-Century Britain: God,
Self, and Other* (Cambridge University Press, 2018). On the *Enquiry
concerning the Principles of Morals*, see especially Annette C. Baier,
'*Enquiry concerning the Principles of Morals*: Incomparably the Best?',
in Elizabeth S. Radcliffe (ed.), *A Companion to Hume* (Blackwell
Publishing, 2008), pp. 293–320, and also Jacqueline A. Taylor (ed.),
Reading Hume on the Principles of Morals (Oxford University Press,
2020). On Hume's contributions to 'criticism', a good point of
departure is Peter Jones, 'Hume on the Arts and "The Standard of
Taste": Texts and Contexts', in David Fate Norton and
Jacqueline A. Taylor (eds), *The Cambridge Companion to Hume*,
second edition (Cambridge University Press, 2009), pp. 414–46.

Politics

The most important study of Hume's political thought remains
Duncan Forbes, *Hume's Philosophical Politics* (Cambridge University
Press, 1975). Essential context is provided by H. T. Dickinson, *Liberty
and Property: Political Ideology in Eighteenth-Century Britain*
(Methuen, 1977), and J. G. A. Pocock, *The Machiavellian Moment:
Florentine Political Thought and the Atlantic Republican Tradition*
[1975], Princeton Classics edition (Princeton University Press, 2016).
A reliable, brief account is given by Knud Haakonssen, 'The Structure
of Hume's Political Theory', in Norton and Taylor (eds), *The
Cambridge Companion to Hume*, pp. 341–80. Paul Sagar, *The Opinion
of Mankind: Sociability and the Theory of the State from Hobbes to
Smith* (Princeton University Press, 2018) contains a rich and
provocative examination of Hume's theory of political obligation.

Hume's contribution to the 18th-century British debate about the politics of party is well described in Max Skjönsberg, *The Persistence of Party: Ideas of Harmonious Discord in Eighteenth-Century Britain* (Cambridge University Press, 2021). On the elements of Hume's political economy, see Andrew Skinner, 'Hume's Principles of Political Economy', in Norton and Taylor (eds), *The Cambridge Companion to Hume*, pp. 381–413, and also Margaret Schabas and Carl Wennerlind, *A Philosopher's Economist: Hume and the Rise of Capitalism* (University of Chicago Press, 2020). A powerful interpretation of Hume's writings on commerce is developed in essays collected in Istvan Hont, *Jealousy of Trade: International Competition and the Nation State in Historical Perspective* (Harvard University Press, 2005). Nicholas Phillipson, *David Hume: The Philosopher as Historian* (Penguin, 2011) is an elegant treatment of Hume's intentions as a historian, usefully supplemented by Tom Pye, 'Histories of Liberty in Scottish Thought, 1747–1787', Ph.D. dissertation, Cambridge University, 2018. See also the essays in Mark Spencer (ed.), *David Hume: Historical Thinker, Historical Writer* (Pennsylvania State University Press, 2013); and Roger L. Emerson, 'Hume's Histories', in *Essays on David Hume, Medical Men and the Scottish Enlightenment* (Ashgate, 2009), pp. 127–54.

Religion

The best general guide to Hume on religion is still J. C. A. Gaskin, *Hume's Philosophy of Religion*, second edition (Macmillan, 1988). For a condensed and updated version of Gaskin's interpretation, see his 'Hume on Religion', in Norton and Taylor (eds), *The Cambridge Companion to Hume*, pp. 480–513. On the Scottish context, see Thomas Ahnert, *The Moral Culture of the Scottish Enlightenment 1690–1805* (Yale University Press, 2014). On the wider 18th-century British debates about revealed and natural religion, see the two chapters by M. A. Stewart in Haakonssen (ed.), *The Cambridge History of Eighteenth-Century Philosophy*, pp. 683–730. Strong claims are made about the 'irreligious' agenda of the *Treatise* in Paul Russell, *The Riddle of Hume's* Treatise: *Skepticism, Naturalism, and Irreligion* (Oxford University Press, 2008). Useful background for Hume's discussion of miracles is provided by David Wootton, 'Hume's "Of Miracles": Probability and Irreligion', in M. A. Stewart (ed.), *Studies in the Philosophy of the Scottish Enlightenment* (Oxford University Press, 1990), pp. 191–229. A summary of philosophical debate concerning 'Of Miracles' is provided by Peter Millican, 'Twenty Questions about Hume's "Of Miracles"', *Philosophy* 68 (2011): 151–92. As a way into the *Dialogues*, Norman Kemp Smith's introduction to his 1935 Oxford University Press edition has worn well. See also Andrew Pyle, *Hume's* Dialogues concerning Natural Religion*: A Reader's Guide* (Continuum, 2006). A good answer to the question of what Hume might have meant when he talks about 'true religion' is given by Don Garrett, 'What's True about Hume's "True Religion?"', *Journal of Scottish Philosophy* 10 (2012): 199–220. Help with understanding Hume's intentions in *The Natural History of Religion* is provided by Richard Serjeantson, 'David Hume's *Natural History of Religion* (1757) and the End of Modern Eusebianism', in Sarah Mortimer and John Robertson (eds), *The Intellectual Consequences of Religious Heterodoxy 1600–1750* (Brill, 2011), pp. 267–95; and Jennifer Smalligan Marušić, 'Refuting the Whole System? Hume's Attack on Popular Religion in *The Natural History of Religion*', *The Philosophical Quarterly* 62 (2012): 715–36.

Index

For the benefit of digital users, indexed terms that span two pages (e.g., 52–53) may, on occasion, appear on only one of those pages.

Hume

Index

EXISTENTIALISM
A Very Short Introduction
Thomas Flynn

Existentialism was one of the leading philosophical movements of
the twentieth century. Focusing on its seven leading figures,
Sartre, Nietzsche, Heidegger, Kierkegaard, de Beauvoir,
Merleau-Ponty and Camus, this *Very Short Introduction* provides
a clear account of the key themes of the movement which
emphasized individuality, free will, and personal responsibility
in the modern world. Drawing in the movement's varied
relationships with the arts, humanism, and politics, this book
clarifies the philosophy and original meaning of 'existentialism' -
which has tended to be obscured by misappropriation. Placing
it in its historical context, Thomas Flynn also highlights how
existentialism is still relevant to us today.

GERMAN PHILOSOPHY
A Very Short Introduction
Andrew Bowie

German Philosophy: A Very Short Introduction discusses the idea that German philosophy forms one of the most revealing responses to the problems of 'modernity'. The rise of the modern natural sciences and the related decline of religion raises a series of questions, which recur throughout German philosophy, concerning the relationships between knowledge and faith, reason and emotion, and scientific, ethical, and artistic ways of seeing the world. There are also many significant philosophers who are generally neglected in most existing English-language treatments of German philosophy, which tend to concentrate on the canonical figures. This *Very Short Introduction* will include reference to these thinkers and suggests how they can be used to question more familiar German philosophical thought.

www.oup.com/vsi

KEYNES
A Very Short Introduction
Robert Skidelsky

John Maynard Keynes (1883–1946) is a central thinker of the twentieth century, not just an economic theorist and statesman, but also in economics, philosophy, politics, and culture. In this *Very Short Introduction* Lord Skidelsky, a renowned biographer of Keynes, explores his ethical and practical philosophy, his monetary thought, and provides an insight into his life and works. In the recent financial crisis Keynes's theories have become more timely than ever, and remain at the centre of political and economic discussion. With a look at his major works and his contribution to twentieth-century economic thought, Skidelsky considers Keynes's legacy on today's society.

SCOTLAND
A Very Short Introduction
Rab Houston

Since Devolution in 1999 Scotland has become a focus of intense interest both within Britain and throughout the wider world. In this Very Short Introduction, Rab Houston explores how an independent Scottish nation emerged in the Middle Ages, how it was irrevocably altered by Reformation, links with England and economic change, and how Scotland influenced the development of the modern world. Examining politics, law, society, religion, education, migration, and culture, he examines how the nation's history has made it distinct from England, both before and after Union, how it overcame internal tensions between Highland and Lowland society, and how it has today arrived at a political, social and culture watershed.

Houston's survey is clear and certainly concise.

Clare Beck, The Scotsman

THE MEANING OF LIFE
A Very Short Introduction
Terry Eagleton

'Philosophers have an infuriating habit of analysing questions rather than answering them', writes Terry Eagleton, who, in these pages, asks the most important question any of us ever ask, and attempts to answer it. So what is the meaning of life? In this witty, spirited, and stimulating inquiry, Eagleton shows how centuries of thinkers - from Shakespeare and Schopenhauer to Marx, Sartre and Beckett - have tackled the question. Refusing to settle for the bland and boring, Eagleton reveals with a mixture of humour and intellectual rigour how the question has become particularly problematic in modern times. Instead of addressing it head-on, we take refuge from the feelings of 'meaninglessness' in our lives by filling them with a multitude of different things: from football and sex, to New Age religions and fundamentalism.

'Light hearted but never flippant.'

The Guardian.